NIKON Z8

for Beginners

Capture Every Moment with Precision and Unlock New
Creative Possibilities with the NIKON Z8's Superior Imaging
and Advanced Performance.

JORDAN M. WALES

TABLE OF CONTENTS

CHAPTER ONE
INTRODUCTION

The release of the Nikon Z8 represents an excellent opportunity for Nikon fans who have invested in the Nikon ecosystem to obtain a new camera. While some people call it the "mini Z9," this camera has almost all of the great features of Nikon's top model at a less expensive price.

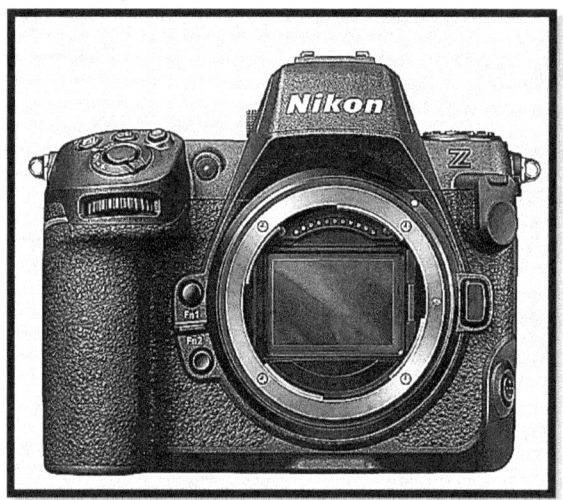

The Z8 camera's sturdy magnesium metal construction gives it a classic appearance, and the curved handle makes it comfortable to hold even during long shooting sessions. It has large knobs and simple settings that allow users to customize their experience and unleash their digital creativity, but the Z8's beauty extends beyond its appearance. Its advanced 45.7MP stacked CMOS camera captures light with precision and dynamic range. When combined with the lightning-fast EXPEED 7 image engine, this camera unlocks a plethora of creative possibilities. In addition to its camera features, the Z8 provides access to Nikon's extensive ecosystem of Z lenses, which were specifically designed to work with its features and suit a variety of artistic concepts. This important release represents a significant step forward for Nikon. It brings them closer to competing with large corporations such as Sony and Canon by providing them with a powerful, professional-grade full-frame mirrorless camera that is ideal for shooting in all situations. One of the most important improvements in the Nikon Z8 is its autofocus ability. The Z8 has a new and improved focusing system that uses deep learning technology. This new feature makes it easier to find subjects and track them in 3D, including tracking animal eyes automatically, which makes the camera even better. Notably, the Z8 does exceptionally well in low light, with autofocus working at an amazing -9 EV, far exceeding its competitors and guaranteeing clear focus even in tough circumstances. Although the Nikon Z8 is great at focusing, it does well when it comes to shooting videos. This camera is ideal for filmmakers and content creators seeking the highest quality and most options. It can record 8K/60p and 4K/120p videos in N-RAW, ProRes RAW, and N-Log formats. Furthermore, the Z8 is an excellent choice for photographers because it lacks a standard mechanical shutter. Instead, it features a stacked sensor design with extremely fast reading speeds. The lack of a motorized shutter reduces the likelihood of rolling shutter effects, keeps the camera in good condition, and allows you to shoot RAW bursts at speeds of up to 20 frames per second. This new concept not only improves the user experience but also allows shooters to be more creative when capturing important moments with precision and clarity. Photographers can rely on the Z8 to capture every detail with incredible clarity and accuracy, whether they're shooting close-ups or doing a lot of trimming in post-processing. This makes the Z8 a versatile tool that can handle the needs of a variety of photography activities.

Specifications

Below are the key specifications of the camera;

Sensor and Processor

Stacked BSI CMOS sensor with 45.7MP: The Nikon Z8 Mirrorless Digital Camera includes a 45.7MP BSI stacked CMOS sensor in an FX-format. This sensor has a great mix of sharpness, fast reading times, great clarity, and very little noise. Its stacked sensor design helps to lower the rolling shutter and its BSI rating means that noise levels are better at the highest ISO settings (32–102400). The Nikon Z 8 is the perfect combination camera for shooters who require a professional camera for shooting in detailed settings and also want to record video at up to 8K resolution. It has a 45.7MP resolution and a full-frame sensor.

EXPEED 7 Picture Processor: The stacked sensor and the EXPEED 7 processor work together to provide extremely fast autofocus, burst shots, a large buffer, smooth video playback, and overall excellent handling. It can shoot at 20 frames per second in raw, 30 frames per second in JPEG, 60 frames per second in 19MP JPEGs with a DX area, and an incredible 120 frames per second in 11MP stills. All of these speeds enable full AF/AE performance. It can store more than 1000 raw images in a burst, allowing it to record raw image loops for approximately 50 seconds. If you enable Pre-Release Capture, the camera will begin the burst before the release action (button half-pressed), and it will last approximately one second before the button is released. With a maximum shutter speed of 1/32,000 sec, an electronic shutter allows you to work in the brightest conditions and with larger apertures. To keep up with faster continuous shooting rates, the focusing calculations are performed at 120 frames per second. HEIF files can be saved using the Nikon Z8 Mirrorless Digital Camera Body, which is a welcome change from JPEG files. When viewed on a display that supports HLG, this 10-bit format provides 1 billion more colors than JPEG while maintaining the same file size.

Electronic Shutter

For all shooting settings on the Nikon Z 8 Camera, only the electronic shutter is used because of its speed and stacked sensor design. You can record at speeds of up to 1/32000 sec, and the stacked structure makes motion blur very small. Also, allowing the camera to shoot an accurate picture of things that move quickly, like cars, golf clubs, and baseball bats. When the mechanical shutter is taken off, this camera can be used without making any noise, and you don't have to worry about the mechanical shutter breaking. The sound of the shutter can be added and the volume can be changed if you still want to hear it when you take pictures.

Intelligent AF

- **Phase-Detection AF with 493 Points**: The famous 493-point phase-detection AF system covers the entire sensor, providing fast and accurate AF that stands out. The fast connection of the Z interface and the fast sensor, which allows for AF readings at up to 120 frames per second, is beneficial to this system. The focusing method is also suitable for working in low light conditions, such as at night, astrophotography, or at shows. The Starlight Mode allows you to focus down to -9EV, making this possible. The Z8 also has 3D Tracking AF, which works with subject recognition to lock on to subjects moving quickly and erratically in both directions. It also has three Dynamic-Area AF modes, allowing you to capture a variety of moving subjects. These modes offer a variety of focus area sizes.
- **Deep Learning Technology with the Ability to Detect Subject Easily:** Subject Detection has become much more advanced thanks to the algorithms and deep learning technology that were brought over from the Z 9. These are different types of subjects, like people, animals, bikes, cars, and now airplanes. Subjects will be found and tracked across the frame instantly in Auto-Area AF

3

mode. Then, in eye detection mode, the camera is set up to find human and animal eyes in the picture and follow them across the screen for more accurate results.

Video Capability

- **Internal recording in 8K60 and 4K120:** The Nikon Z8 Mirrorless Digital Camera offers a range of frame rates and resolutions up to 8K. When the true 24p frame rate is used, both 8K and 4K resolutions are supported. This gives it a movie-like appearance, and you can record in 4K UHD. Oversampled UHD 4K video at up to 60p is possible in an 8K area, increasing image sharpness and clarity. The camera can also capture high-resolution frame grabs from 8K and 4K movies, which can be used to create 33MP or 11MP stills.

- **Video Shoot in 12-bit N-RAW and ProRes RAW**: Internal 12-bit raw recording at up to 8.3K 60p in Nikon's N-RAW format, which makes files smaller. This format is available, as well as internal ProRES WAR HQ. It is possible to record N-RAW at up to 8.3K at 60p or 24p, 4.1K at up to 120p, 5.3K at up to 60p with a 1.5x crop, or 3.8K at 120p with a 2.3x crop. You can also record in ProRes RAW at up to 4.1K and 60p.

- **10-bit recording with ProRes and H.265**: You can record internally with 10-bit color and 4:2:2 sampling for the ProRes 422 HQ and H.265 codecs, as well as H.264 and 4:2:0 color. You can also change the color freely, and it also has 10-bit N-Log and Flat Color character settings.

Professional body design that is smaller

- **Design that is sleek, modular, and long-lasting:** The Z8 is viewed as the D850's successor, whereas the Z9 is regarded as the smaller successor. The Nikon Z8 is 15% smaller than the D850, and 30% smaller than the Z9. The Z8 is much smaller in size than the Z9, which includes a built-in battery grip. With a smaller and lighter body, the Z 8 is now suitable for daily use. It's also ideal for mounting or using a gimbal for video work. Synchro VR now supports in-body vibration reduction. When used with specific Z lenses, this can reduce camera shaking by up to six stops.

- **Real-Time Viewfinder:** The EVF has a 3.96m-dot OLED screen with a customizable brightness of up to 3000cd/m2 and an improved Real-Live Viewfinder. With the High fps mode, the Viewfinder can have an update rate of up to 120 fps, which makes the picture look more natural and smooth.

- **LCD with four-axis tilt**: The Nikon Z8 Mirrorless Digital Camera has a 3.2-inch, 2.1 million-dot, four-axis tilting touchscreen LCD. This makes it easy to take pictures from high or low angles.

Connectivity

The Nikon Z8 also includes some connectivity options to meet various workflow requirements. This is consistent with the professional-grade build quality. These include a full HDMI port for video output, a 3.5mm headphone jack for monitoring audio, and mic jacks for connecting external microphones. There are two built-in USB-C ports. The first is for transfers and connections, while the second is for power delivery and battery charging. A 10-pin port allows you to connect a variety of tools and devices from afar. With built-in Bluetooth and Wi-Fi (2.4 and 5GHz), you can wirelessly transfer files and control the camera from a mobile device. This is also compatible with the NX Mobile Air app, which is designed for managing files.

Features

Screen and Viewfinder

The Nikon Z8 has an excellent camera and screen setup, which is very similar to the Z9. It has a great electronic viewfinder with 3.69 million dots and 0.8x zoom, allowing you to see what you're doing even while shooting continuously. A small frame around the sample image indicates that the camera is actively capturing, providing the photographer with real-time feedback.

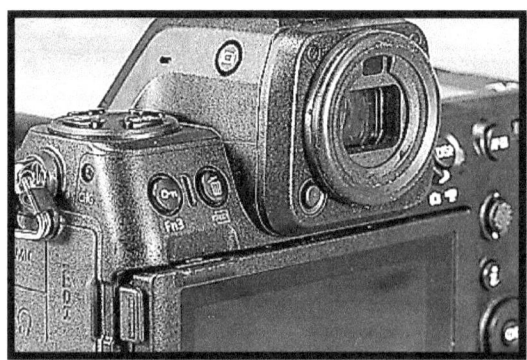

Nikon simulates color processing, exposure spanning a range of +/-3 EVs, and depth of field down to apertures as narrow as f/5.6. However, users can change these settings through the View Mode (photo LV) menu, which includes color neutralization, turning off exposure preview, and improving shadow visibility. This lets photographers make the display work like an optical viewfinder and suit their needs. Customizable buttons let you quickly switch between preview settings. This is especially helpful in high-contrast scenes like sunsets, where dark shadow details might get blurred. Landscape photographers can create a dedicated button for previewing depth of field effects with smaller apertures. The camera also includes exposure and composition tools such as a live histogram display, electronic levels, gridlines, and more. The Z8 features the same 3.2-inch screen as the Z9, with a resolution of 2.1 million dots. The screen is unique in that it has four hinges that allow it to tilt vertically and horizontally, making it suitable for both low angle and overhead shooting. This is a significant improvement over the Z7 II, giving photographers more options than ever before. However, unlike a side-hinged screen, it cannot rotate.

ISO and Noise

The Z8's 45.7MP sensor outperforms most full-frame cameras, which have 61MP sensors. It stands out. At ISO 64, there is no noise, and even at ISO 1600, a close examination of files on the screen reveals faint hints of brightness noise. Small details become less clear as ISO 6400 is increased, but noise does not begin to affect image quality until ISO 25,600. However, you should avoid ISO 51,200 and 102,400 because they add a lot of noise and little useful dark data.

Buffer Rates

In general, professional photographers value double memory card slots in their cameras. These slots offer a useful backup option as well as the ability to store an excessive number of photos, giving photographers peace of mind if a card fails during important shoots. The Nikon Z8 partially addresses this need by having two card slots, but only one of them supports the lightning-fast CFexpress format. The other slot, however, can only accept UHS-II cards. The Nikon Z8 is a powerful camera ideal for high-speed photography situations such as wildlife photography, sporting events, and photojournalism. It can shoot bursts of over a thousand RAW images at an incredible 20 frames per second using a high-speed CFexpress card, demonstrating how quick and agile it is. However, the fact that it requires an SD card slot for backup or primary storage makes it slower. Even if you don't always need to shoot at 20 shots per second or faster, being able to do so without restriction is critical for professionals who have to deal with unpredictable shooting conditions. Relying on the slower SD card slot can make the camera significantly less useful, especially when quick, continuous shooting is required.

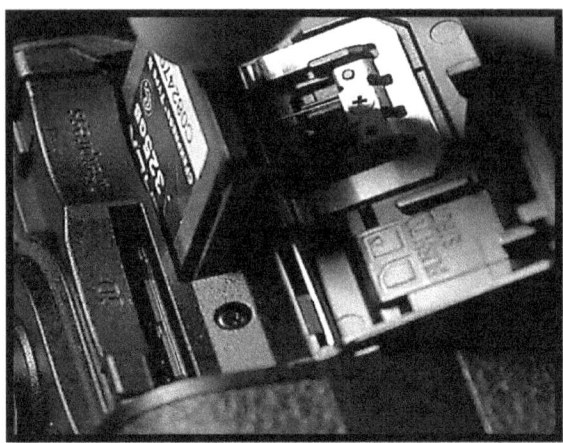

Also, while the CFexpress slot is great for high-speed and efficient shooting, using an SD card as a backup could slow things down. Because of this, users need to carefully think about their shooting and workflow and figure out how to best use the camera's two memory card slots, weighing the benefits of having two options against the possible limitations of the slower storage.

Autofocus

Subject recognition tracking has become a key area of improvement in camera technology in recent years, and Nikon's implementation in the Z8 (and Z9) is among the best. This feature allows the camera to detect and lock onto various subjects, such as people, animals, or vehicles, and gives users the option of prioritizing specific subjects or allowing the camera to select them automatically. For photographers who enjoy capturing/shooting with a single focus, such as those photographing planes at an airshow, instructing the camera to focus on specific subjects while ignoring others is extremely useful. However, most of the time, leaving the system on Auto is sufficient because it allows the camera to correctly identify and track subjects on its own. Identified subjects are highlighted in the viewfinder, making it simple to make a decision when there are multiple options. When the subject recognition system has difficulty identifying subjects, the camera seamlessly switches to its standard focusing system, which provides users with a variety of focusing options. Users can adjust the size of the focus points, which include three sets of squares that can be positioned anywhere in the frame to meet their compositional requirements. Also, Nikon's 3D tracking feature allows the camera to follow moving subjects.

Shooting in Wildlife

Wildlife photographers often need to use higher ISO settings than photographers of other subjects. With the Nikon Z8's updated processor and sensor, you can confidently raise the ISO without encountering distracting noise. The high-resolution 45.7-megapixel sensor and the cutting-edge EXPEED 7 chip work together to deliver exceptional noise performance, making sure that your images stay clear and detailed even in low light.

Movie Recording

The Nikon Z8 is a great choice for professional filmmakers because it can shoot in 8.3K 60p RAW and 4K 120p RAW, giving them a lot of options for post-production. Interestingly, Nikon promises up to 90 minutes of continuous shooting in 8K 60p without overheating, which is better than competitors in terms of cooling efficiency. This improved cooling mechanism is what sets it apart from others in its field.

Shooting Cinematic Video

If you want to make videos that look like they were shot in a movie theater, the Nikon Z8 is a great camera for you. It can record 8K video at up to 60 frames per second, which gives you amazing clarity and detail and lets you play back videos in slow motion without any problems.

The camera also records in 4K at 120 frames per second, allowing you to create high-quality slow-motion sequences with speeds reduced by up to five times. This feature, like those found in the Nikon Z9, allows filmmakers to capture captivating moments with accuracy and artistic flair. Along with these great video resolutions and frame rates, the Nikon Z8 allows you to record in RAW format, giving you complete control over image quality and editing options. With resolutions of up to 8.3K at 60 frames per second or 4.1K at 120 frames per second, filmmakers can easily change their footage to fit their creative vision. To get the most out of these recording features, you need to make sure that the memory cards you use are compatible and can handle the high data rates that come with these resolutions and formats. The camera supports several recording formats, including Apple ProRes RAW and H.265, allowing filmmakers to select the ones that work best for them. The Nikon Z8 also has numerous features that make filmmaking easier and more enjoyable. For example, it has an HDMI output for external monitoring, focus peaking for precise focusing, and zebras to control exposure. The ability to simulate 2x optical zoom expands filmmakers' creative options by allowing them to capture dynamic shots without the need for additional lenses or equipment. The Nikon Z8 can record continuously for up to 90 minutes in 8K resolution, allowing you to shoot for longer periods without stopping. This, combined with its advanced features and high-quality images, makes the camera a useful and reliable tool for filmmakers who want to create professional-quality movie content.

Shooting in Dark Environments

In comparison to other camera models, they perform well in low light. For example, the Nikon Z9 has a DxO score of 2451, while the Sony A7R V has a score of 3400. These high scores indicate that there is little noise even at ISO settings that match these numbers. The Nikon Z8 also has backlit buttons, making it easier to use in low-light environments. When combined with the appropriate lenses, it can focus down to an incredible -9 EV, ensuring clarity even in low light.

CHAPTER TWO

FIRST-TIME CAMERA SET UP

You can quickly start using this camera, with just a few simple steps for proper setup: charging the battery, attaching the lens, inserting a memory card, and setting the clock. However, for those who are new to using a camera, it is vital to become proficient in navigating the menu button, command dials, and touch screen to accurately set up your camera for the first time:

Buttons and Controls needed for setting your Camera Up

Before using your Z8 camera, there are a few tasks you need to complete. These tasks involve operating various camera buttons and controls, such as the multi-selection pad and the MENU button. **Now, we'll go into each control necessary for setting up your camera and understanding its functionalities:**

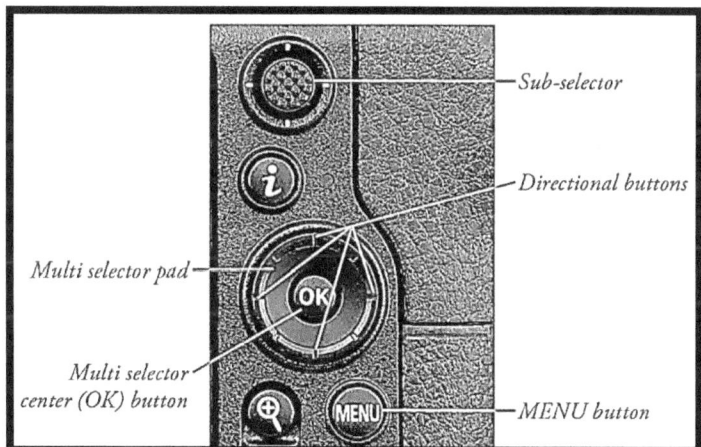

- **The Menu Button**: Conveniently positioned on the left of the LCD panel, this button simplifies menu navigation with a single touch. Pressing it again can either exit the menu or confirm a selection, depending on the context.
- **The Multi-Selector**: Similar to controls on various point-and-shoot cameras, this device includes a central button and well-sized controls for directional inputs (up, down, left, right). It also functions when pressed at an angle. The multi-

selector is typically used for navigating menus, selecting focus points, scrolling through images, and adjusting display settings.

- **The Center of the Multi-Selector Button**: This button works with the right navigation icon to select menu options, often replacing the dedicated "OK" button on the camera's left side. Its functionality can be customized for different tasks depending on the situation.
- **The "OK" Button**: For consistency, the "OK" button usually performs the enter function instead of the multi-selector center button. Its primary functions, such as toggling card locations during playback, are fixed and cannot be reassigned.
- **The Sub-Selector Control**: Mainly designed for setting the focus point, this control can also be customized for menu navigation. It can be pressed inward to lock focus or exposure.
- **The Main Command and Sub Command Dials**: Located at the front and rear of the Z8, these dials are crucial for adjusting camera settings. The main command dial primarily controls shutter speed, while the sub-command dial modifies secondary settings. In Manual exposure mode, the sub-command dial adjusts the aperture, and the main command dial controls the shutter speed. These dials are functional when the Z8's exposure meter is active. If the meter is dormant, pressing the shutter release button will reactivate it, allowing the use of the main and sub-command dials.

Using the Touch Screen during Setup

Your camera's tilting LCD offers a wide range of touch functionalities, making it an adaptable tool for a variety of tasks. Whether you're a seasoned pro or just getting started, the touchscreen on your camera is an indispensable asset for setting up your camera and navigating through playback or live view modes. Here is a breakdown and a detailed overview of the various functions available on the touch screen:

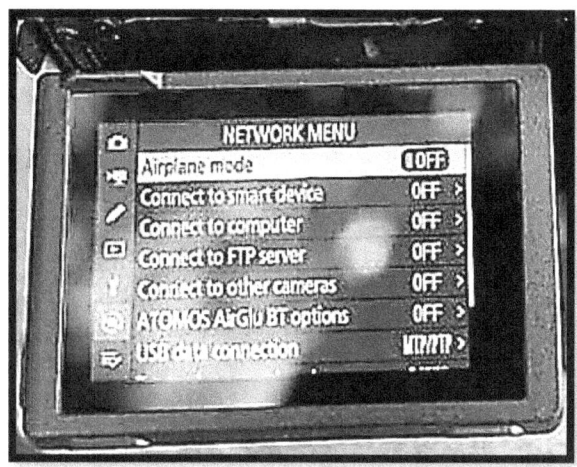

The above picture is an image of the touchscreen

1. **Playback Mode**:
    - ○ **Image Navigation**: Browse through images effortlessly using swipe gestures during playback.
    - ○ **Zooming**: Adjust the magnification level on the screen easily for a closer look at images.
    - ○ **Moving the Magnified Area**: Change the position of the zoomed-in area by swiping your finger on the display.
    - ○ **Thumbnail and Movie Access**: Navigate through thumbnails and movies smoothly by interacting with the screen.
2. **Live View Mode (LVM)**: This feature allows you to view and capture images using the camera's LCD screen, offering a convenient way to compose shots and make real-time adjustments like a professional:
    - ○ **Capture Photos**: Touch the display to capture an image in Live View mode, eliminating the need to press the shutter button.
    - ○ **Focus Point Selection**: In Live View and Movie modes, select a focus point by simply tapping on the touch screen.
    - ○ **Adjusting White Balance**: Select a specific region on the display to compute the white balance.
3. **Shooting Mode**:
    - ○ **Menu Navigation**: Navigate through menu options in Shooting Mode using the touchscreen controls, bypassing the traditional multidirectional button.
    - ○ **Text Input**: Use the on-screen keyboard for efficient text input, making it easier to enter copyright information in the Setup menu compared to using traditional controls.

You can personalize or completely turn off touch features, limiting them to playback functions if desired. The Touch Controls option allows for the customization of full-frame playback "flicks" in various directions. Additionally, the Touch Shutter/AF function can be turned off while using Live View and recording videos, providing more flexibility and control.

4. **Mastering Touchscreen Gestures**:
   o **Flick**: A smooth swipe across the screen with one finger allows you to navigate to the next or previous images during playback.
   o **Slide**: Move within a magnified image using a single finger to navigate in any direction.
   o **Stretch/Squeeze**: Adjust the size of an image by using two fingers to expand or contract it while viewing.
   o **Tap**: Use your finger to interact with the display, make selections, customize settings, or choose the focus point as needed.

Now that you understand the touch controls and gestures, you can proceed to fully set up your camera and start using it by following the steps in the subsequent sections.

How to Set the Language

The Z8 camera offers support for a wide range of languages, making it accessible and user-friendly for people all over the world. Considering that distributors often customize the camera's **language settings based on the region, it's probable that it's already localized accordingly. If you want to change the language settings, just follow these steps:**

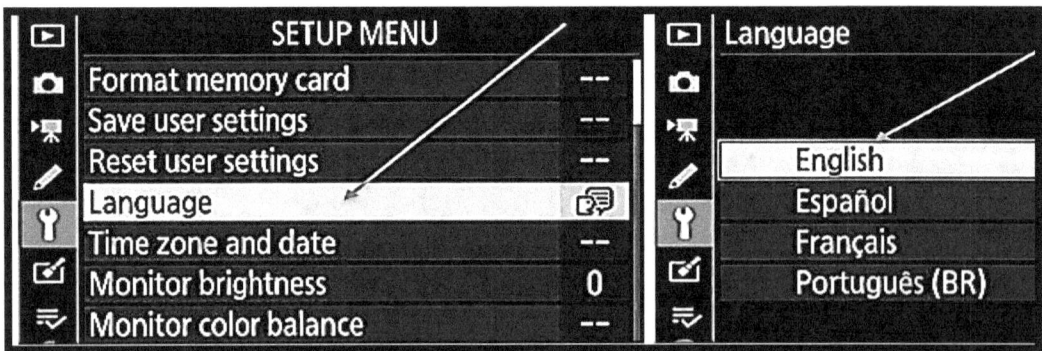

* **Accessing the Setup Menu**: Start by locating the Setup Menu on your Z8 camera. This menu is the central hub for a wide range of configuration options.

- **Choosing the Language Option**: Navigate to the Setup Menu and find the Language option. Scroll through the menu to locate this option or any other settings you need.
- **Choosing the Right Language**:
    o Use the circular Multi-selector pad at the rear of the camera to navigate through the list of available languages. Move up, down, left, and right to browse through the options.
    o Once you've identified the language you want to use, select it by pressing either the OK button at the bottom left of the camera or the Multi-selector center button in the middle of the Multi-selector pad.

How to Set the Time Zone and Date

Make sure your Z8 camera location reflects the accurate time zone for a seamless camera experience; here are the step-by-step instructions to set the correct time zone:

1. **Go to the Setup Menu:** Go to the Setup Menu screen flow and choose the third screen. Note; keep in mind that this menu is the go-to menu for adjusting and fine-tuning all the settings on your camera.

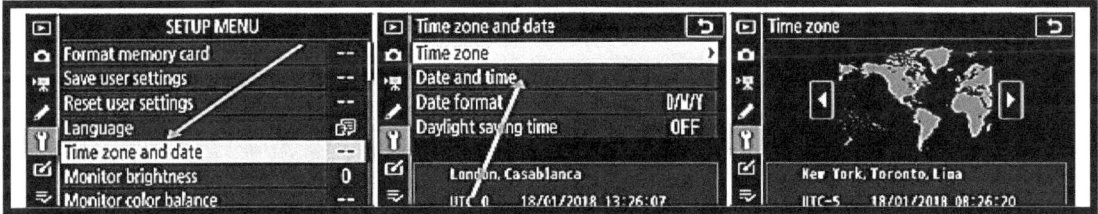

2. **Adjusting the Time Zone:**
- - Use the Multi Selector pad to navigate and see your current location highlighted in yellow. This information will help you determine the appropriate time zone configuration. To indicate the selected time zone, a vertical yellow stripe or a faint yellow outline will be displayed, along with a red dot. Make sure the time zone is displayed correctly in the bottom-right corner of the screen.
- -After you've selected the correct time zone, click the OK icon to confirm your choice. By completing this step, your camera's time will be perfectly aligned with the time zone of your current location. Once you've set the time zone, it's time to move on to the next steps and get that date and time exactly right.
3. **Setting up the Date and Time:**

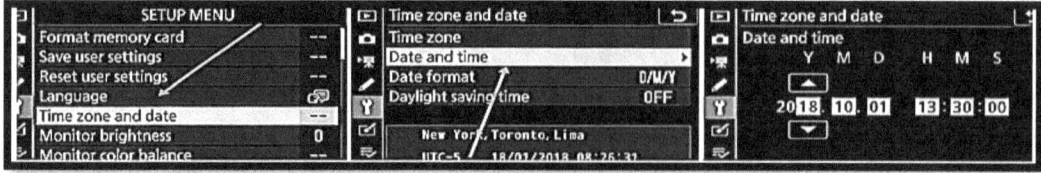

- Choose the third screen again within the Setup Menu screen flow.
- - Use the Multi Selector pad to easily navigate between sections with dates and times. Use vertical or lateral navigation to change the relevant parameters. To ensure accuracy, the time values are displayed in 24-hour military time format. Once you've entered the date and time accurately, click the OK button to confirm your settings. Note: Your camera's internal clock must be synchronized with the specified date and time in the selected time zone.

4. **Adjusting Date and Time Format:**

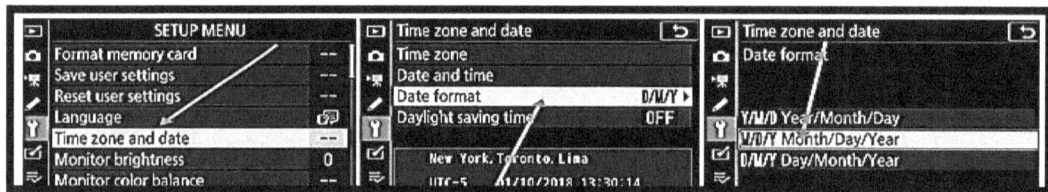

- Once again, go to the Setup Menu and find the third screen.
- Utilize the Multi Selector pad to effortlessly navigate and select your preferred date format from the array of options.
- Press the OK button to confirm your selection and customize the date and time display to your desire.

How to Charge and Insert a Battery into the Camera

To ensure smooth shooting sessions, keep your Nikon Z8 camera's battery fully charged at all times. Proper power management is essential for capturing uninterrupted shots. When you insert the battery into the MH-25a charger, a flashing indicator light will show that the charging process has begun. This pulsating light illuminates for approximately 2.5 hours, indicating that the battery is being charged. After the battery is fully charged, the status indicator will stay continuously illuminated to notify you that the charging cycle is complete.

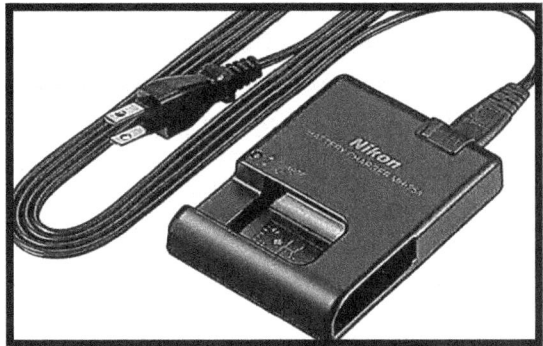

Once the charging process is finished, the next step is to carefully insert the battery into the camera. To do this, you can simply open the lever found on the bottom of the camera, which will grant you access to the battery compartment.

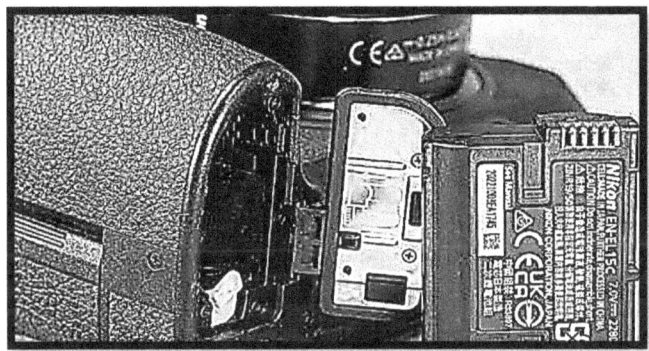

It's important to properly insert the charged battery in your Z8 camera to ensure it's ready for operation. This way, you can capture incredible images and videos without any interruptions.

Mounting Your Lens

When preparing to use your Nikon Z8 camera with a chosen lens, handle it carefully and ensure it is securely attached while keeping it safe. Begin by carefully removing the lens from its packaging, and keeping the rear lens cover on for added protection against dust and scratches. Simply insert the lens vertically into the designated compartment within the camera case to keep it safe and convenient for quick access. This not only provides easy access but also protects against unintentional harm or accidents.

The cover protects the rear portion of the lens until it is ready to be attached, allowing for a quick and secure transition when needed. To remove the body cover, simply rotate it away from the release mechanism and remove the rear lens cover and body cap, setting them aside for later use. Let's now move on to the lens installation process. Align the raised white protrusion on the lens mount with the corresponding marking on the lens barrel. Rotate the lens until it securely clicks into place, aligned with the direction of the shutter release button. Certain lenses, especially telephotos and those with swiveling collars for tripod attachment may need extra care when being installed. For a perfect fit, make sure to adjust the collar to avoid any collisions between the tripod foot and the camera's prism front overhang.

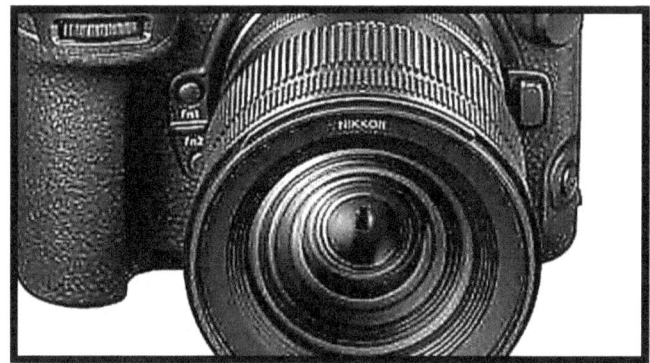

After attaching the lens, change the focus mode to M-AF or AF to enable autofocus functionality. You can easily detach and reattach the lens hood by reversing the lens and adjusting the "petals" to face outwards. This setup enhances the portability of the lens and hood combination by reducing unwanted light flare and protecting the front portion of the lens from any disturbances.

Adjusting the Diopter Control as Needed

For those who are well-versed in the world of photography, even minor changes to the viewfinder can significantly improve their ability to capture the perfect shot. However, if you already wear contact lenses or glasses, you may find that the diopter correction settings do not require any adjustments. However, for those who prefer to use the Z8 without glasses, the camera includes a built-in diopter adjustment feature that ranges from -2 to +1. This adjustment allows users to easily fine-tune the focus through the viewfinder for crystal-clear images. For optimal vision adjustment, simply focus your eye on the subject through the viewfinder and rotate the diopter adjustment dial next to it until the image appears sharp and clear. It's crucial to keep in mind that when evaluating focus through the viewfinder, it's best to rely on the actual image rather than the status indicators. This is because the distance between the focus screen and the indicators outside the image region may vary slightly, which can impact the accuracy of your focus assessment.

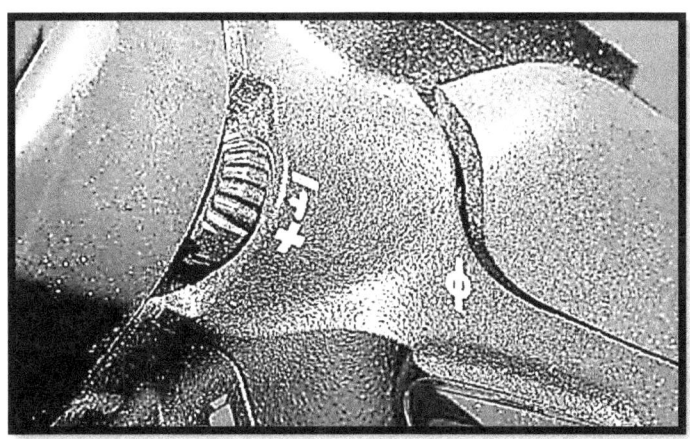

When multiple users use the same camera and have different diopter preferences, it's a good idea to keep track of the changes made. This feature allows users to easily return to their preferred diopter setting without the need for readjustment. By carefully observing the number of touches and rotations required to switch between users, you can optimize the process of adjusting for different users' visual needs. In addition, if the standard diopter correction range is insufficient for your needs, Nikon offers nine different diopter-adjustment viewfinder correction lenses for the window. These lenses provide additional customization options, with prices ranging from around $16 to accommodate diopter adjustments up to +3. This feature allows users to easily customize their viewing experience to match their individual visual preferences, ensuring clear and comfortable photography sessions.

Inserting a Memory Card

Knowing the proper procedure for inserting or removing a memory card from your camera is necessary to prevent any potential damage or loss of data. **Here's a comprehensive guide on how to safely insert memory cards with your camera:**

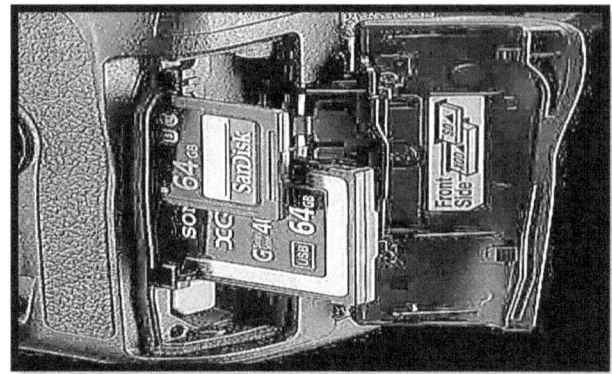

1. Begin by opening the memory card cover. To do this, gently slide the door on the back-right side of the camera towards the rear of the device and open it with caution.
2. Ensure the camera is turned off and the memory access indicator, which indicates if the card is being written to, is not lit. This precaution is required to avoid any potential data corruption or loss.
3. The memory card area has two slots: an XQD card slot at the bottom and an SD media slot at the top.
4. Insert the XQD card with the label facing towards the back of the camera. Insert the card into the opening first, with the edge that contains the contacts. This ensures precise alignment and a seamless connection.
5. Insert the card carefully and smoothly, ensuring proper alignment and a secure click into place.

Follow the steps below to remove your memory card from your camera;

1. When pulling out a memory card, it's important to make sure that the camera is turned off or that the memory access indicator is not illuminated.
2. Thereafter, locate and take out the memory card you want to remove. If it's an XQD card, just press it inward and it will pop out, making it easy for you to remove.
3. Keep in mind that it is important to handle the card with care to prevent any damage to the contacts or the card itself.
4. But when removing an SD card, gently push it inward until it pops out, and then carefully pull it out of the slot.

How to Format a Memory Card

Formatting a memory card for your new camera is easy with these two simple methods:

1. **Formatting through the Setup Menu:**

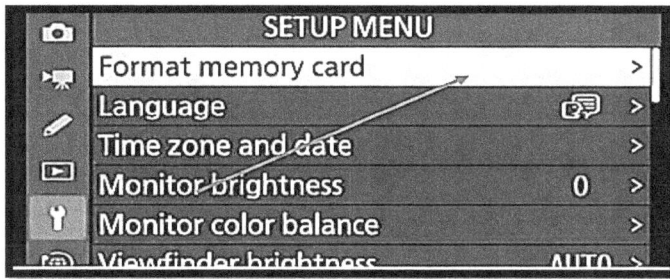

- Click on the menu button and go to the Setup Menu. Use the multi-selector to browse to the Format Memory Card option.
- Select the SD or XQD memory card to format.

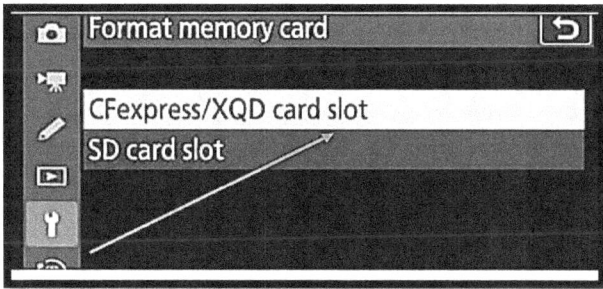

- Make sure to click Yes to confirm your selection.
- Alternatively, you can access the Setup menu by pressing the wrench icon using the control next to the LCD.
- Press the OK button to initiate the formatting process.
2. **Transferring files to your computer:**
- - When transferring image files from a memory card to a computer using a card reader or cable, the card's content is removed.
- -Unfortunately, this method cannot delete protected files or identify and prevent access to the card's damaged sections.
- To completely erase the contents of a card and start from scratch, it is recommended to format it (as shown above).

- -This method can still be used for preserving or sharing images on the card.

CHAPTER THREE

CAMERA CONTROLS, BUTTONS AND FEATURES

Top Side Controls, Buttons and Features

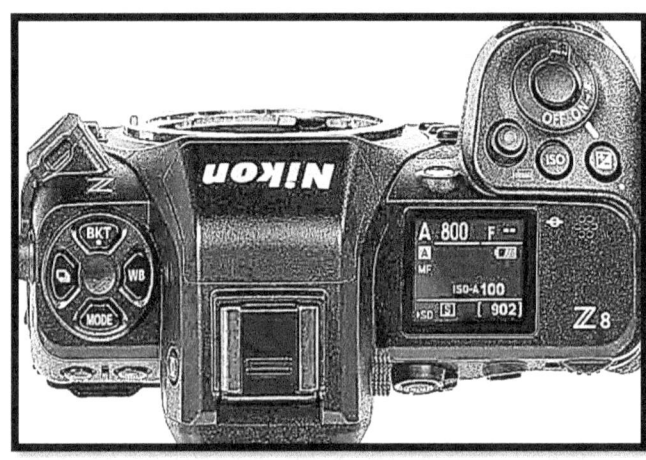

1. **BKT Bracket Button**: To bracket shots, use the BKT button along with the Main Command Dial and Sub-Command Dial. This combination allows you to select the number of pictures and adjust the brightness variation between each frame.
2. **WB Button to Change White Balance**: Press the WB button to access the white balance settings. Then, turn either the Main Command Dial or the Sub-Command Dial to adjust the white balance to your preference.
3. **Mics with Two Channels for Making Videos**: The camera's stereo microphones are essential for recording high-quality audio during video sessions, enhancing the overall viewing experience.
4. **Button to Record Video**: In video mode, use the "video record" button to easily start and stop recording, ensuring you capture every moment.
5. **Shutter Release Button**: Half-press the shutter release button to initiate focusing, and fully press it to take a picture. This provides precise control over when to capture images.
6. **Switch to Turn Power On and Off**: The On/Off button controls the camera's power state, allowing you to quickly switch between active and sleep modes as needed.

7. **ISO Button to Change ISO**: To adjust the ISO setting, press the ISO button and turn the Main Command Dial. This helps you adapt to different lighting conditions for optimal brightness.

8. **Button for Exposure Compensation**: Use the exposure compensation button and the Main Command Dial together to fine-tune exposure settings, ensuring accurate and balanced exposure levels in your photos.

9. **Speaker for Audio Output**: The camera's speaker allows you to playback recorded sounds or listens to camera settings and alerts.

10. **Control Panel to Show Settings**: The control screen displays the camera's preset settings, providing quick access to important information for shooting.

11. **Diopter Adjustment for Clearer Viewfinder**: The diopter adjustment lets you modify the lens focus to match your eyesight, ensuring clear and comfortable viewing.

12. **Button for Monitor Mode**: The monitor mode button allows you to switch between the camera and monitor screens, enabling you to choose the one that best suits your shooting needs.

13. **Button for Shooting Modes**: To change shooting modes, press the mode button and turn the Main Command Dial. Available modes include Programmed Auto, Aperture Priority, Shutter Speed Priority, and Manual.

14. **Release Mode Button for Shooting Speed**: Adjust the release mode setting by using the release mode button and the Main Command Dial together. This provides more control over shot speed and timing.

Back Side Controls, Buttons, and Features

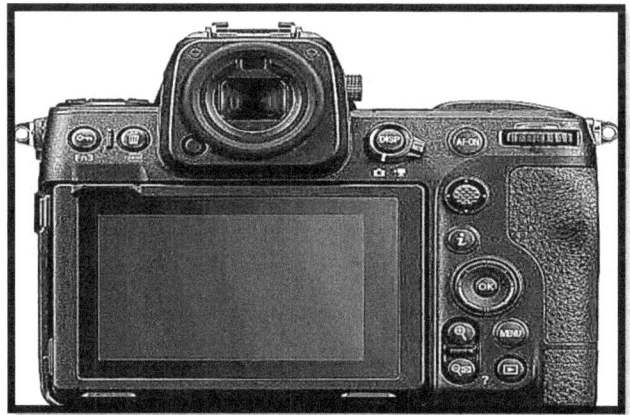

The following is a list of what the back controls on your camera do:

1. **Eye Sensor for Display Toggle**: When your eye is detected in the viewfinder, the eye sensor automatically switches the display from the monitor to the viewfinder, allowing seamless transitions between viewing options.
2. **DISP Button for Display Navigation**: Press the DISP button to cycle through different display panels. This enables you to adjust the screen information according to your needs and shooting style.
3. **Photo/Video Selector Button**: This button allows you to easily switch between photo and video modes, providing quick access to your desired shooting mode.
4. **Sub-Selector Joystick for Focus Point Selection**: Use the sub-selector joystick to choose the focus point, offering precise control over focus and exposure. Press and hold to lock the focus and brightness settings when needed.
5. **AF-ON Button for Autofocus Activation**: Press the AF-ON button to activate autofocus, ensuring quick and accurate focusing on your subject before taking a picture.
6. **Main Command Dial for Parameter Adjustment**: The main command dial allows you to adjust camera settings such as aperture, shutter speed, and exposure, providing greater flexibility and control over your shots.
7. **iButton for Menu Access**: Pressing the iButton opens the camera's menu settings, where you can customize and adjust settings to fit your needs. The options available may vary depending on the camera mode.
8. **OK Button for Confirmation**: Press the "OK" button to confirm selections or settings, ensuring that changes made in the camera's menu system are correctly applied.
9. **Multi-Selector for Navigation**: Use the multi-selector button to navigate through menus or select focusing points, facilitating easy and quick menu navigation and focus selection.
10. **Magnify Button for Image Enlargement**: Press the magnify button to enlarge the image on the LCD screen, allowing for a closer and more detailed inspection.
11. **Menu Button for Menu Access**: Press the menu button to access the camera's menu system, where you can adjust a variety of settings and personalize the camera to your preferences.
12. **Zoom-Out Button for Viewing Images**: The zoom-out button enables you to reduce the size of the current image on the LCD screen, providing a better overview of your captured images for thorough review and evaluation.
13. **Playback Button for Image Review**: Press the playback button to immediately view the most recent image taken on the LCD screen, facilitating quick review and assessment of photos while shooting.

14. **Trash Button for Deleting Images**: Use the trash button to delete the current image from the LCD screen, allowing for easy removal of unwanted photos from the camera's memory.

15. **Protect/Fn3 Button for Image Protection**: Press the Protect/Fn3 button to safeguard the current image during playback, preventing accidental deletion or modification. Additionally, use this button in conjunction with the Main Command Dial to set Picture Controls, granting precise control over image quality and style settings.

Controls, Buttons, and Features on the Front Side

Here is a list of the buttons and controls on the front of the camera and what they do:

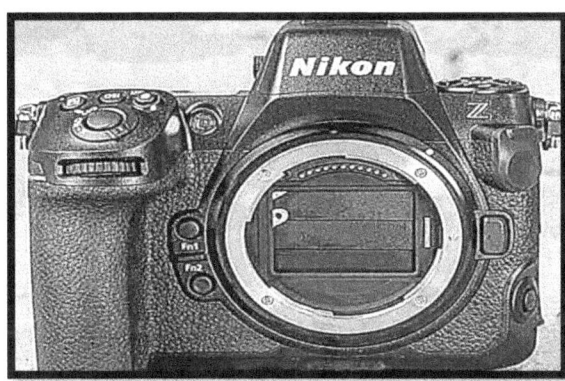

1. **Sub-Command Dial to Adjust Settings**: The sub-command dial allows you to modify various camera settings, offering greater flexibility and control during shooting.

2. **10-Pin Remote Terminal (Below the Lid)**: Located under the cover, the 10-pin remote terminal is where additional remote controls can be connected, enabling remote release and control of the camera.

3. **Connector for External Microphone (Under the Side Cover)**: This port, found under the side cover, allows for the connection of external microphones, improving audio quality when recording videos or audio.

4. **Headphone Jack for Audio Monitoring**: The headphone jack, concealed on the side of the camera, allows you to connect external headphones for real-time audio monitoring, ensuring sound quality and volume are as desired.

5. **HDMI Connector (Under the Side Cover)**: The HDMI port, located under the side cover, allows you to connect an HDMI cable, enabling high-definition video output to external devices or monitors.

6. **USB Data Connector for Transferring Data**: Found under the side cover, the USB data port allows for the connection of a data cable to transfer files and data between the camera and a computer or other compatible device.

7. **USB Power Plug for Power Supply**: Also under the side cover, the USB power port supports a USB power supply cable, keeping the camera powered during extended shooting sessions or data transfers.

8. **Focus Mode Button to Choose Focus Mode**: Press the focus mode button to access and adjust the focus mode settings. Then, use the Main Command Dial to make changes that fit your shooting needs and preferences.

9. **Battery Chamber Cover for Inserting the Battery**: The battery chamber cover provides access to the camera's battery compartment, ensuring secure and easy insertion of the battery for continuous shooting.

10. **Fn2 Button**: The Fn2 button can be customized for specific functions, such as selecting the "Choose Image Area" option, providing quick access to frequently used features or settings.

11. **Fn1 Button**: The Fn1 button can also be assigned a specific function or setting; by default, it accesses the "Shooting Menu Bank," giving users flexible control over the camera's operation to match their shooting styles.

12. **Memory Card Slots**: Located under the side cover, the memory card slots accommodate memory cards for storing photos and videos, offering ample storage capacity for all your camera needs.

The Viewfinder Display (Photo)

When you take a picture, the viewer gives you important information that will help you get the perfect shot:

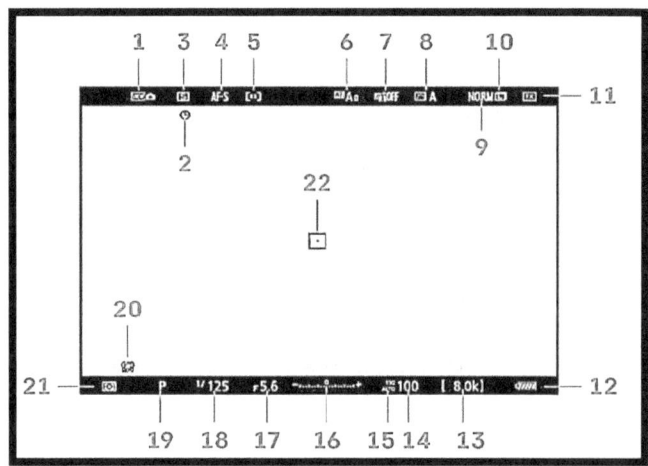

1. **View Mode Display:** Here, you will see the current view mode so you can change the settings to get the greatest viewing.
2. **Sign that the clock is not set:** The flashing Clock Not Set Indicator lets you know that the date and time have not been set, so your pictures have correct timestamps.
3. **Details about the release mode:** This displays the current release mode, which helps you select the right shot method for the result you want.
4. **Focus Mode Display:** This tells you the current focus mode, which will help you get your subject in perfect focus.
5. **Indication for the AF-Area Mode:** The screen shows the AF-area mode, which lets you choose the best focus area for your design.
6. **White Balance Setting**: The white balance setting is shown in the camera, which makes sure that the colors in your pictures are correct.
7. **Status of active D-lighting:** A light that lets you know if Active D-lighting is on or off helps you set the brightness so that the lighting in your scenes is even.
8. **Preview of the Picture Control:** The present Picture Control setting is shown, which lets you see how the image's colors and tones will look.
9. **Information about image quality:** The file format and compression level are shown by the picture quality setting, which could be JPEG, RAW, or RAW+JPEG.
10. **Size of the image shown:** The viewer displays the current image's size, which lets you know about the file's quality and size.
11. **Image Area Indicator:** This number shows the current picture area and can tell the difference between full-frame (FX) and cropped sensor (DX) modes.
12. **Battery Level Indicator:** The battery display lets you know how much power is left in the battery, so you never miss a shot because the battery is low.
13. **Number of Remaining Exposures:** The number of exposures left is shown, which shows you how many more pictures you can take with the current settings and the amount of room on your memory card.
14. **Display for ISO Sensitivity:** The most recent ISO setting is shown, which lets you change the sensitivity to get the best picture in different lighting situations.
15. **Indicator for ISO/Auto ISO:** An icon lets you know if Auto ISO is on, which changes the sharpness automatically as the light changes.
16. **Indicator for exposure and exposure compensation:** Showing the current exposure settings and the state of exposure correction makes it possible to finetune the exposure levels.
17. **Display of the Aperture Value:** The present aperture setting is shown, which lets you change the depth of field and the amount of light coming in for artistic effects.

18. **Information about shutter speed:** The shutter speed is shown in the camera, so you can change the settings to blur motion or freeze action as needed.
19. **Indication of Shooting Mode:** The method of recording is shown for quick reference, such as Programmed Auto (P), Aperture Priority (A), Shutter Priority (S), or Manual (M).
20. **Indicator for Vibration Reduction**: A light shows if the shaking reduction is on or off. This feature makes pictures clearer, especially when there isn't much light.
21. **Display for Metering Mode:** The present metering mode is shown, which helps you choose the right exposure measuring method for the correct exposure reading.
22. **Display of the Focus Point:** The chosen focus point is shown, which helps you get clear pictures by focusing on the subject precisely.

Viewfinder Display (Movie)

When you're making a movie, the camera gives you important information and visual cues to help you do it.

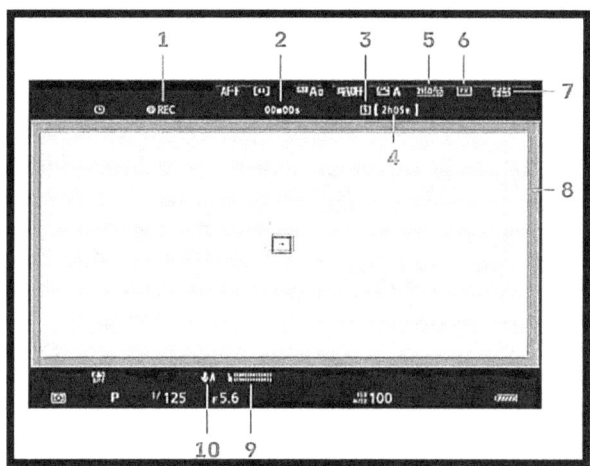

- **Recording Indicator**: This light shows whether a video is currently being recorded or if the recording is off, making it easy to see the camera's recording status at a glance.
- **Video Recording Time**: The screen displays the duration of the ongoing video recording, helping you keep track of the elapsed time since the recording started.
- **Destination**: Indicates where on the memory card the video is being saved, ensuring you always know the storage location of your videos for easy retrieval.

- **Remaining Recording Time**: Provides an estimate of the remaining recording time based on current settings and available space on the memory card, aiding in better planning of your sessions.
- **Frame Rate and Size**: Displays the frame rate and size of the video being recorded, allowing you to adjust settings to achieve the desired video quality.
- **Picture Area**: Shows the current picture area format, such as DX or FX, providing information about the sensor crop factor for your video recording.
- **Video File Type**: Indicates the type of video file being created, ensuring compatibility with editing software and playback devices.
- **Recording Indicator**: A red border around the display serves as a prominent indicator, letting you know when the camera is recording video.
- **Sound Level**: Displays the audio levels being captured by the camera's microphone, allowing you to monitor and adjust sound levels during recording.
- **Microphone Sensitivity**: This shows the current sensitivity settings for the camera's microphone, enabling you to adjust audio input levels for optimal sound quality.

Monitor Display (Photo)

While you're taking a picture, the screen gives you different kinds of information to help you.

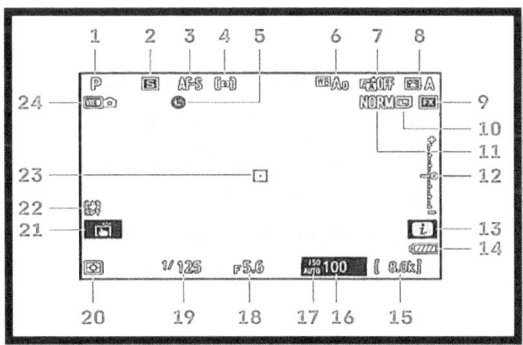

- **Shooting Mode**: Displays the current shooting mode of the camera, helping you adjust settings to achieve your desired shooting style.
- **Release Mode**: Indicates the current release mode, informing you how the camera will shoot, such as taking a single shot or continuous shots.
- **Focus Mode**: Shows the current focus mode, assisting you in achieving perfect focus on your subject.

28

- **AF-Area Mode**: Displays the current autofocus area mode and provides details about the selected focus point on the camera.
- **Clock Not Set Indicator**: A flashing "clock not set" indicator alerts you to set the date and time for accurate timestamps on your photos.
- **White Balance**: Displays the current white balance setting, ensuring accurate color reproduction in your photos.
- **Active D-Lighting**: Indicates whether Active D-Lighting is enabled or disabled, helping you control dynamic range and brightness for well-balanced photos.
- **Picture Control**: Shows the current Picture Control setting, allowing you to see how the image's color and tone will appear.
- **Picture Area**: Displays the current picture area format, such as FX or DX, informing you about the camera crop factor for your shot.
- **Picture Size**: Indicates the current picture size setting, providing information about the quality and file size of your photos.
- **Picture Quality**: Displays the current picture quality setting, such as RAW, RAW+JPEG, or JPEG, ensuring optimal image quality.
- **Exposure and Exposure Compensation Indicator**: Shows the current exposure settings and indicates whether exposure compensation is enabled, allowing you to adjust exposure levels.
- **i Symbol**: Tapping the "i" icon opens the "i Menu," giving you quick access to additional camera settings and options.
- **Battery Level Indicator**: Displays the remaining battery power, ensuring you never miss a shot due to a drained battery.
- **Number of Exposures Remaining**: Shows the number of remaining shots based on current settings and available memory card space.
- **Auto ISO Indicator**: Indicates whether Auto ISO is enabled, allowing automatic adjustment of ISO sensitivity for various lighting conditions.
- **ISO Sensitivity**: Displays the current ISO sensitivity setting, enabling you to adjust brightness levels for optimal image quality.
- **Aperture**: Shows the current aperture value, allowing you to control the depth of field for creative effects.
- **Shutter Speed**: Displays the current shutter speed setting, enabling you to adjust brightness and motion blur.
- **Metering Mode**: Indicates the current metering mode, helping you select the appropriate exposure measurement method for accurate exposure readings.
- **Touch Shooting**: Indicates whether Touch Shooting is enabled, allowing you to control focus and capture shots with a simple touch.

- **Vibration Reduction Indicator**: Displays whether Vibration Reduction is enabled, reducing camera shake for sharper images, especially in low-light conditions.
- **Focus Point**: Shows the selected focus point, helping you ensure sharp focus on your subject.
- **View Mode**: Displays the current view mode, providing information about the camera's display setup for reviewing and composing photos.

Monitor Display (Movie)

The monitor screen shows the following important information for shooting a movie:

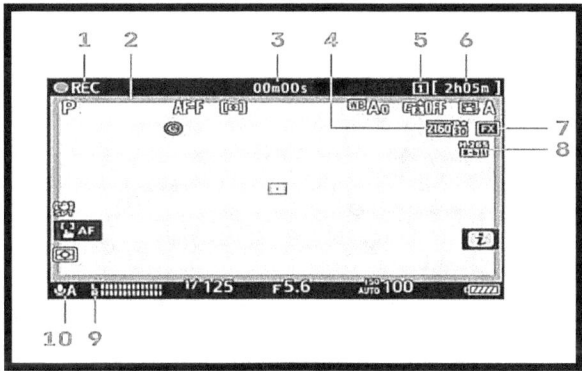

- **Status of Recording (Enabled or Disabled)**: This light indicates whether a movie is being recorded or if the recording is off, providing a clear view of the camera's recording status.
- **Indicator for Recording**: A red border appears around the screen when the camera is recording video, making it obvious that the recording is in progress.
- **Video Recording Time**: Displays the duration of the ongoing video recording, helping you monitor how much time has elapsed since the recording started.
- **Rate of Frames and Size**: This shows the current frame rate and dimensions of the video being recorded, informing you about the video's quality and clarity.
- **Destination**: Indicates where on the memory card the video is being saved, ensuring you always know where to find your videos for easy access.
- **Remaining Amount of Time**: Provides an estimate of the remaining recording time based on the current settings and available memory card space, helping you better plan your sessions.
- **Picture Area**: Displays the current picture area format, such as FX or DX, and informs you about the sensor crop factor for your video recording.

- **Type of Video File**: Indicates the type of video file being created, ensuring compatibility with editing tools and viewing devices.
- **Level of Sound**: This shows the audio levels being picked up by the camera's microphone, allowing you to monitor sound levels while recording.
- **Sensitivity of the Microphone**: Displays the current sensitivity settings for the camera's microphone, enabling you to adjust the audio input for optimal sound quality.

Control Panel

During shooting, the control box shows you important information and data that will help you with your photography:

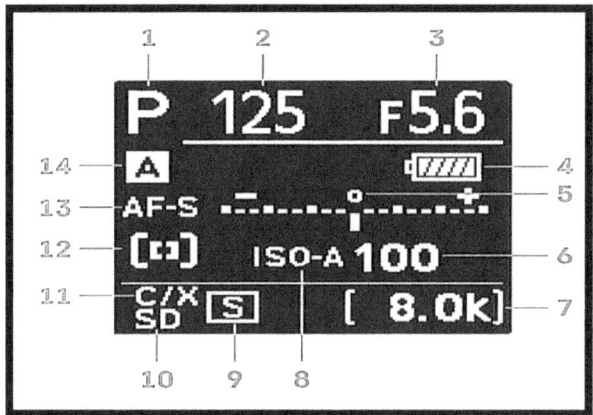

- **Shooting Mode**: Displays the currently selected shooting mode, providing insight into how the camera is configured for capturing images.
- **Shutter Speed**: Indicates the duration the camera's shutter remains open during exposure, showing the current shutter speed setting.
- **Aperture**: Shows the current aperture setting, which affects the depth of field and the size of the lens opening.
- **Battery Level Indicator**: Provides the current battery charge level, so you know how much power remains for continued shooting.
- **Indicator for Exposure**: Displays how the current exposure settings are impacting the image brightness, assisting you in achieving the correct exposure.
- **ISO**: Shows the current ISO setting, which indicates the camera's sensitivity to light.

31

- **Amount of Exposure and Recording Time**: Provides information on the number of remaining photos or videos that can be captured based on the current settings and available memory card space.
- **ISO Indicator of Sensitivity**: Displays if Auto ISO is enabled, which automatically adjusts the ISO sensitivity according to the lighting conditions.
- **Release Mode**: Shows the current release mode setting, detailing how the camera's shutter release is configured.
- **SD Card Memory Slot (2)**: Indicates which SD card slots are being used for storage, helping you track where your photos are saved.
- **CFexpress/XQD Memory Slot (1)**: Shows which CFexpress or XQD card slots are set for storage, providing options for high-speed data transfer.
- **Indicator for AF-Area Mode**: Displays the current autofocus area mode, assisting you in focusing accurately on your subject.
- **Focus Mode**: Indicates the current focus mode setting, allowing you to adjust how the camera focuses.
- **Shooting Menu Bank**: Shows which shooting menu bank is currently selected, facilitating quick access to your custom shooting settings.

CHAPTER FOUR

OVERVIEW OF SOME QUICK BASIC NIKON SETTINGS AND OPERATIONS TO IMMEDIATELY START USING YOUR

Camera as a Beginner

Once you are certain that the memory card is inserted into the camera, the battery is completely charged, and the time and date are set properly, you may begin snapping images. This section will walk you through the process of configuring basic camera functions so you can begin shooting images and videos straight away.

Overview of the Exposure Compensation

The camera simplifies brightness adjustments by including both Program and Auto modes. Although these automated modes work well in most situations, there are times when manually adjusting the camera's exposure is necessary to achieve the desired result. It turns out that exposure compensation is an effective tool for dealing with unusual lighting conditions. Assume your topic is in front of a stark white background. In some situations, the camera's default settings may result in underexposure due to the brightness of the background. In this case, exposure must be taken into account. This control, conveniently located next to the multi-selector wheel's Right button, displays positive and negative numbers with small plus and minus signs against black and white backgrounds, respectively. Using this tool, photographers can manually adjust exposure settings to suit their preferences, ensuring that the subject is properly exposed even in difficult lighting conditions.

When in Program mode, focus on the subject and activate the Right button, the screen displays a vertical scale with exposure compensation values shown from +2.0 at the top to -2.0 at the bottom. The exposure compensation amount can be changed in a variety of ways, including using the command dial, spinning the multi-selector dial, or pressing the Up and Down keys. A yellow check mark indicates the scale's adjusted value; moving the checkmark in different directions results in brighter or darker visuals. The camera's LCD instantly switches from dark to bright to show how exposure was changed before taking the picture, allowing users to see the results of their changes immediately. Furthermore, a bar graph on the left side of the display provides a visual representation of lighting values, allowing photographers to make more informed decisions about exposure adjustment. To avoid unintended consequences on future images, reset exposure correction to zero after taking the original photo. Users should proceed with caution, however, because exposure correction settings are retained even when the camera is turned on and off. As a reminder of any changes made to the exposure settings, the adjusted value is still displayed in the bottom right corner of the screen next to the exposure compensation symbol.

Overview of the Motion Picture Recording

Using the Motion Picture Recording helps to record high-quality movies

1. Accessing Movie Mode
- **Switch to Movie Mode**: Ensure the flash is off (the flash unit button should be off). Press both the Left and Menu buttons simultaneously to access the Movie Mode icon. Navigate through the menu and confirm your selection by pressing the Right button.

2. Frame Rate Selection
- **Choose Frame Rate**: In the Movie Mode menu, select the appropriate frame rate for your video. Options typically include:
  - **25 frames per second (25p/50p)**
  - **30 frames per second (30p/60p)**
  - Choose based on regional standards (NTSC or PAL) and the desired speed and quality of your video.

3. Selecting Video Quality
- **Set Video Quality**: Choose the video resolution from available options:
  - **Full HD (1080p)**
  - **Ultra HD (4K)**
  - Higher resolutions offer more detail but require more memory and processing power. Select based on your camera's capabilities and your intended use.

4. Setting up Autofocus Mode
- **Autofocus Options**: For clear focus during video recording, choose between:
  - **Full-time AF**: Continuously adjusts focus.
  - **Constant AF**: Maintains focus on a stationary subject.

5. Additional Settings
- **Enhance Recording**: Activate additional features as needed:

- o **Zoom Microphone**: Improves audio quality.
- o **Electronic VR (Vibration Reduction)**: Enhances video stability.

6. Starting to Record
- **Begin Recording**: Tap the red Movie button on the rear of the camera to start recording. A short blackout occurs, followed by the display of the remaining recording time and a red "REC" light. Tap the red button again to stop recording.

7. Verifying Autofocus Mode
- **Check Autofocus**: If using Full-time AF, press the OK button or navigate to the next page to verify the autofocus settings. This mode will adjust focus dynamically during recording.

8. Maintaining Stability
- **Avoid Shaky Footage**: Steady the camera to ensure smooth footage. Use a tripod or monopod for stability, and incorporate controlled camera movements for capturing wide scenes effectively.

Overview of the Fully Automatic Auto Mode

For users who would rather make a few settings changes, auto mode is a practical option since it lets the camera take care of the majority of the job. This is how to switch on auto mode:

1. Prepare the Camera
- **Remove the Lens Cap**: Take off the lens cap securely and store it in a safe place.

2. Power On
- **Turn On the Camera**: Press the On/Off Control to power up the camera. The LCD screen will activate, indicating that the camera is on.

3. Set Auto-Shooting Mode
- **Select Auto Mode**: Turn the mode dial on top of the camera until the white indicator lines up with the green camera symbol. This sets the camera to auto-shooting mode.

4. Configure Focus Mode
- **Set Autofocus**: Ensure that the AF (Autofocus) setting is selected on the focus mode switch located above the AE/AF Lock button on the rear of the camera.

5. Adjust Image Quality
- **Access Shooting Menu**: Use the directional buttons next to the Menu icon on the rear of the camera to navigate to the Shooting Menu.
  - o **Image Size**: Choose **1680x3456** for the best quality.

- o **Image Quality**: Select **Fine** for high-quality images.
- o **Resume Shooting**: Press the Menu button to save settings and exit the menu.

6. Compose Your Shot
- **Use Viewfinder or LCD Screen**:
  - o **LCD Screen**: Rotate or move the screen to adjust its position.
  - o **Viewfinder**: Press the Monitor button to switch back to the viewfinder.

7. Adjust Diopter
- **Clear Vision**: Turn the diopter dial on the left side of the lens to achieve clear vision through the viewfinder.

8. Turn on the Flash
- **Activate Flash**: Press the lightning bolt button next to the built-in flash unit on the left side of the camera.

9. Set Flash Mode
- **Choose Flash Mode**: Press the Up button on the multi-selector to bring up the flash mode menu and select **Auto** mode.

10. Focus and Zoom
- **Compose the Shot**: Use the LCD screen or viewfinder to frame your subject.
- **Adjust Zoom**: Use the Zoom Lever surrounding the shutter button:
  - o **Zoom Out**: Move left for a wider view.
  - o **Zoom In**: Move right to get a closer view.

11. Take the Photo
- **Focus**: Partially press the camera release button. The successful focus will be indicated by green squares and a buzzer sound. If a red square appears, adjust the camera and press the shutter button halfway again.
- **Capture the Image**: Hold the shutter button down to take the picture.

Note: Remember that you have greater control over your images in Program mode, but the camera still controls the lighting.

Additionally, this is how to switch on Program Mode: Make the appropriate mode dial switch to enter Program Mode. Pressing the Menu button will bring up further options. The Shooting menu in Program Mode has four screens, each with twenty programmable choices such as exposure bracketing, ISO, metering mode, and white balance. In Program mode, the camera also uses the shutter speed in addition to the aperture to calculate exposure.

Basic Overview of the Focus Function

Selecting the right focusing mode is important to getting crisp, clear photos. Press the Down button (usually shown on your camera's display as a flower symbol) to start the focusing mode.

When you press it, a little menu with three options appears:

- The AF Method, denoted by the initials "AF," is a commonly used focusing technique for most shooting scenarios.
- Use the Macro Mode, represented by a flower emblem, to capture close-up photos of nearby subjects.
- The "Infinity Mode" feature, represented by a mountain symbol, allows for clear images of distant objects and landscapes.
- Each focus setting is designed to adapt to various shooting situations, allowing users to capture high-quality photos in a variety of conditions. For example, the AF Mode is appropriate for everyday photography, the Macro Mode aids in precise close-ups, and the Infinity Mode ensures sharpness when photographing distant objects or expansive landscapes.
- Use arrow keys to quickly select the top icon from the menu. The remaining options will vanish quickly. It is critical to select the correct option (for example, AF) and click the OK button to confirm it. Interestingly, because it is the default option, the AF Mode symbol quickly disappears after selection. Choosing quickly provides instant access to focusing settings and ensures that the camera is ready for the required shooting scenario. The concealed AF Mode indicator simplifies the design while emphasizing how frequently it is used in photography.
- Accessing shooting options. To access the shooting options, press the menu button on the back of the camera. Use the arrow keys to navigate the options until the second screen's AF Area Mode appears in yellow. Click OK, and then select "Manual (Normal)."
- Activate the Fine-tuning Shooting Display by pressing and holding the shutter button halfway after verifying the desired option. Make sure that a directional line-filled box appears. Otherwise, click OK to view them.
- Correctly configuring the shooting display is essential for accurate focus and framing. The focus frame's visual cues aid in image composition. Maintaining the visibility of the vertical lines simplifies navigation through the shooting interface.
- Shifting the Focus Frame Position: The focus frame is initially centered. To move the frame around the screen, use the multi-selector wheel or the directional keys. To secure the center frame, press the OK button.

- To check exposure and focus, align the subject within the white focus guidelines and partially press the shutter button. Focus is confirmed when the focus frames turn green and a buzzer sounds.
- To lock focus on an off-center subject, move the focus frame over it and partially press the shutter button. Press the button halfway and move the camera to your desired location. Take a picture to keep the focus on the original subject.

Basic Overview of the Manual Focus

Manual focus is an important tool for photographers who want to have complete control and accuracy over their shots. Manual focus allows photographers to precisely adjust focus independently, ensuring the best possible sharpness and clarity in their photographs, as opposed to autofocus, which relies on the camera's algorithms to determine focus. This feature is very useful in a variety of shooting situations, especially when there is low light, obstacles such as wire fences or glass barriers, detailed close-ups, or subjects are dispersed at different angles from the camera. To activate manual focus mode, photographers must move the focus mode slider to the MF setting, which is typically located above the AE/AF Lock button on the camera body. When the manual focus mode is activated, the monitor initially displays at the normal magnification level before seamlessly switching to two or four times the normal magnification, giving shooters a better view of the focus region. In manual focus mode, the shot screen becomes the interface's main focal point. Users can fine-tune focus with precision thanks to the convenient buttons located above the aperture and shutter speed indicators, which allow for zoom adjustments. Clear instructions in the bottom left corner guide photographers through the process of adjusting magnification levels and returning the screen to its normal size while manipulating the focusing scale with the multi-selector dial. This ensures focused attention and flawless performance.

When focus is achieved in the macro range, a visual cue in the form of a white bar on the focus scale indicates the progression of focus adjustments by turning bright green. After making focus adjustments, users can confirm the changes and return the screen to its original size by pressing the Down button. As an alternative, you can quickly return the camera to focusing mode by pressing the Right button, which will cause it to focus on the object in the center of the screen without further assistance. Depending on the camera settings, manual focus users can achieve even greater accuracy by using the control ring or side zoom control in addition to the standard controls. With these additional options, photographers can frame their shots more precisely and freely, allowing them to strike a better balance between technical execution and creative vision. Furthermore, the Setup menu's Peaking function offers a plethora of options for those who need extra help focusing. Users can gradually enlarge the white pixels that light up areas of sharp focus by adjusting the command dial's strength and turning on Peaking. This cutting-edge feature makes it much easier to achieve pinpoint focus with unrivaled dexterity, ensuring superb image quality even in the most demanding shooting situations.

How to Capture Images and Record Videos

Capturing Still Subjects

Using Auto Mode

1. **Set to Auto Mode**
   - **Choose Auto Mode**: Turn the mode dial on top of the camera to the (auto) setting. This allows you to capture images with automatic settings.
2. **Check Shooting Screen Information**
   - **Battery Level**: Observe the battery level indicator on the screen to ensure you have sufficient power for shooting.
   - **Remaining Exposures**: Check the number of shots left before the memory card is full.
   - **Toggle Data Display**: Press the (display) button to switch between different data views on the screen.

3. **Camera Handling**
   - **Stabilize the Camera**: Ensure the camera is steady to avoid camera shake.
   - **Avoid Touching Sensitive Areas**: Do not touch the lens, flash, AF-assist illuminator, eye sensor, microphone, or speaker with your fingers or other objects to prevent interference with camera functions.

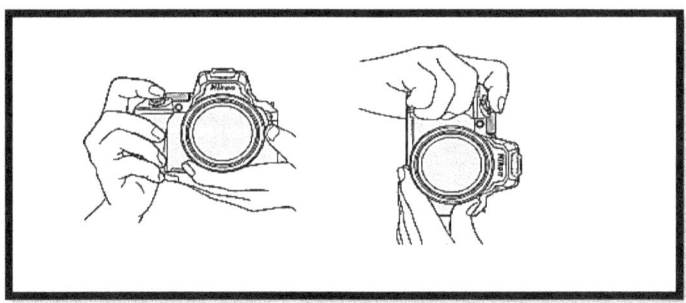

- Frame the image in the way that best suits you
  - o   Use the side or zoom controls to change the zoom.
- To increase stability, think about utilizing a tripod.
- To focus, partially press the shutter-release button.
  - o   Pressing and holding the button until a slight resistance is felt is referred to as "**halfway**".
  - o   The focus area or indicator turns green when the subject is in focus.
  - o   Note: The camera focuses on the middle of the frame when using digital zoom; the focus area is not displayed.
- The camera is unable to focus if the focus area or indicator flashes. Make composition adjustments and try halfway pressing the shutter-release button once more.
- To take the picture, hold down the shutter-release button down without lifting your finger.

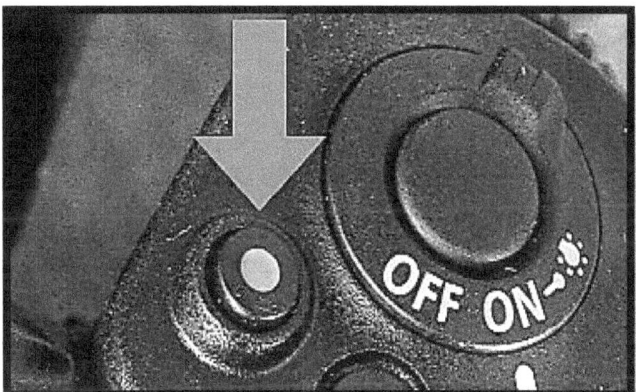

Video Recording

Press the (movie-record) button to start movie recording and bring up the shooting screen display. Once more, press the same button to stop recording. The ability to modify shutter speed and f-number, especially for movie recording, is available when you turn the mode dial to (Movie manual).

How to Review Pictures and Movies

How to Review Pictures

When in Playback Mode

Users can quickly switch to playback mode and review captured images by pressing the dedicated playback button, which is conveniently located on the right side of the LCD screen. This button, which looks like a tiny triangle, is located next to the LCD viewing screen and allows you to easily navigate the picture library. Users can navigate through images sequentially using the motion buttons or the multi-selector dial. Furthermore, the zoom function on top of the camera allows users to enlarge and closely examine specific areas of an image, making it easier to see finer details. Photos taken with the camera's continuous shooting feature display "OK" in the lower left corner, followed by a colon and a triangle. When you click the OK button, a slideshow with a sequence of images starts. The motion buttons allow users to navigate through the series' photos. When you press the "Up" button, the main playback screen appears, giving you easy access to more images and image sequences.

When in Shooting Mode

When the Image Review feature is enabled in the Monitor Settings option of the Setup menu, each still image captured is quickly displayed on the screen or through the viewfinder if one is used. This quick review feature allows users to quickly assess brightness, framing, and focus by providing instant feedback on photos they have taken. Upon capture, the image is shown on the screen for about a second by default, giving you enough time to quickly review it before moving on to the next shot.

How to Play and Review Movies

To begin the cinematic experience, users must first search their photo library for a video file that has the recognizable icon in the lower right corner of the screen. Look for a file name that ends in.mp4, which indicates a recognized video format such as 1080p. Once you've found a video file, you can easily start playing it. Simply click the OK button as a video frame appears on the screen. The film illuminates and appears on the LCD screen or, if an electronic viewfinder is being used, the eyepiece. A row of buttons that resemble DVR buttons is located in the bottom left corner of the screen, making it easy to access various viewing options. To confirm your selection, use the motion buttons to move through the options. To end the selection, press OK. However, the multi-selector dial is useful for those who want more control over playback. The ability to fast-forward by turning this dial right or rewind by turning it left provides users with an additional level of flexibility. It's worth noting that when the camera is connected to a television, the noise level remains constant. In such cases, users must rely on the TV's volume settings to adjust the audio to their preferences.

CHAPTER FIVE

THE Z8 EXPOSURE MODE

Understanding exposure is critical for getting the best shot. Mastering the delicate balance of light control is critical for capturing photographs that accurately capture the subject's subtle details. A solid understanding of exposure is essential for capturing the full spectrum of colors and tones in a scene. A well-exposed image reveals intricate details and produces a vibrant color spectrum, whereas inadequate exposure can result in lost details and overexposed highlights. Mastering the art of exposure is a delicate dance that requires a thorough understanding of how light interacts with the camera's digital sensors. These sensors, while extremely advanced, have some limitations when it comes to capturing the entire range of tones in a given scene. As a result, photographers must make informed decisions to accurately capture the essence of their subject. When it comes to Z-series mirrorless cameras, photographers frequently discuss the "exposure triangle," which consists of aperture, shutter speed, and ISO sensitivity. These three components work together to control the amount of light that reaches the sensor. Adjusting one setting while changing another can aid in maintaining a consistent level of exposure, emphasizing the interdependence of these elements. Nonetheless, each modification has drawbacks. Understanding how aperture and shutter speed work has a significant impact on depth of field and the ability to capture motion in photographs. Just like a photography expert, changing the ISO setting can have a significant impact on the amount of noise in the image. A thorough understanding of these nuances is essential for photographers who want to master exposure. To truly understand exposure, one must investigate the complexities of light. It begins with recognizing the primary light source, whether it is the sun shining brightly, the soft illumination of an indoor lamp, a burst of artificial light, or the dancing flames of a campfire. Then, one should closely follow the path of light as it interacts with the camera, passing through the lens before capturing its essence on the sensor. Essentially, mastering exposure transcends technicalities and becomes an art form that requires a profound understanding of light and its complexities. Understanding the various factors that impact exposure in photography is essential for creating captivating **images. Now, let's explore these factors:**

Understanding and Controlling Exposure in Photography

1. **Intensity of the Light Source**
   - **Impact on Exposure**: Adjusting the intensity of your light source is crucial for achieving the right exposure. Whether dealing with natural sunlight or artificial studio lights, controlling the light intensity can significantly affect the exposure. This can be managed by manually adjusting strobe lights or using diffusers to soften sunlight.

2. **Light Duration**
   - **Continuous vs. Brief Emissions**: Light sources may be continuous or emit light in short bursts (like a flash). Understanding the duration of light emission helps in capturing images accurately, especially in dynamic scenarios. Adjust your settings to ensure the light duration aligns with your desired outcome.

3. **Understanding Light Interaction**
   - **Light's Behavior**: Light interacts with subjects in various ways: reflecting off surfaces, passing through translucent materials, or directly illuminating objects. Mastering these interactions helps in manipulating exposure effectively by adjusting the quantity and quality of light reaching the subject.

4. **Lens Aperture**
   - **Regulating Light Entry**: The aperture controls the amount of light entering the camera. By adjusting the aperture size (measured in f/stops), you can influence exposure. A larger aperture (smaller f/stop number) lets in more light, while a smaller aperture (larger f/stop number) reduces the light entering the camera.

5. **Shutter Speed**
   - **Controlling Exposure Time**: Shutter speed determines how long the camera's sensor is exposed to light. It impacts exposure by controlling the duration of light exposure, which is crucial for capturing motion or long exposure shots. Shutter speeds can range from fractions of a second to several minutes.

6. **ISO Sensor Sensitivity**
   - **Adjusting Sensitivity**: ISO affects the sensor's sensitivity to light. Higher ISO settings increase sensitivity, making the sensor more responsive to low light but may introduce noise. Lower ISO settings reduce sensitivity and are typically used in well-lit conditions for cleaner images.

These variables interact intricately, with changes in one parameter frequently necessitating compensatory changes in another. For example, increasing the aperture size, adjusting the shutter speed duration, or changing the ISO sensitivity all result in an equivalent adjustment in exposure. With a thorough understanding of these relationships, photographers can confidently achieve the desired exposure in a variety of shooting situations. It's important to remember that in some shooting modes, exposure adjustments may not have a direct impact on the final image. This is because the camera automatically adjusts to keep the desired exposure. However, there are alternative ways to adjust exposure in these modes, giving photographers more flexibility and control.

Understanding F/stops and Shutter Speeds

For those familiar with cameras, understanding lens aperture, also known as f/stop, is critical. Consider it a ratio, similar to a fraction, in which the numerical value represents the aperture opening size to the lens' focal length. Understanding the relationship between f/2 and f/4 is crucial in photography. However, the difference is more than just a simple progression; each step represents a significant shift in light transmission. Moving from f/4 to f/2 significantly increases the amount of light entering the camera. This progression is typically defined by a series of intermediate f/stops, each representing a size that is either double or half of the previous one. As a result, a lens' apertures could range from f/4 to f/16, with each step representing a reduction in light. Furthermore, the realm of shutter speeds adds an extra layer of complexity. Shutter velocities are typically expressed in fractions of a second, with the numerator frequently omitted. Take note of numbers like 60, 125, 250, and 500, which represent exposures of 1/60th, 1/125th, 1/250th, and 1/500th of a second, respectively. Manufacturers such as Nikon frequently use quotation marks to indicate longer exposures, which helps to avoid any confusion. Therefore, numbers like 2, 2.5, and 4.0 represent the duration of exposures, which last for 2.0, 2.5, and 4.0 seconds, respectively.

Understanding Equivalent Exposure

Understanding aperture and shutter speed is essential for achieving the ideal exposure in photography, while ISO sensitivity can be adjusted to improve results. This adjustment is critical for achieving the ideal balance of depth-of-field or motion capture. The concept of equivalent exposure is central to this discussion, as it emphasizes that the total amount of light reaching the camera sensor remains constant regardless of the aperture and shutter speed settings. Whether you use a small aperture with a long shutter speed or a wide aperture with a fast shutter, the exposure will remain constant. This principle is critical for photographers who want to ensure consistent exposure levels in various shooting situations.

SHUTTER SPEED	F/STOP	SHUTTER SPEED	F/STOP
1/30th second	f/22	1/1000th second	f/4
1/60th second	f/16	1/2000th second	f/2.8
1/125th second	f/11	1/4000th second	f/2
1/200th second	f/8	1/8000th second	f/1.4
1/500th second	f/5.6		

When using Program (P) mode, the camera's metering system will determine the best exposure settings for you. Photographers who are familiar with cameras can easily achieve different exposures by adjusting the main command dial to show the desired equivalent exposure combination. The "Flexible Program" feature highlights its adaptability by placing an asterisk next to the letter P. By simply rotating the command dial, you can easily adjust depth-of-field and shutter speed, allowing you to exercise creative control in Program mode. It is important to note that this flexibility is not available when using flash photography.

How to Accurately Calculate and Determine Exposure

Understanding how a camera determines focus can help you calculate the proper exposure. We can achieve the best results by following certain principles and making specific assumptions. One important principle to remember is to consider the overall brightness of a scene or a particular area within it. The goal is to adjust the brightness to a neutral gray tone, also known as middle gray, which is usually around 18% gray. However, keep in mind that, while the human eye perceives this as a shade of gray, the camera's calibration typically favors a slightly darker tone. When determining exposure, specific areas of a predetermined pattern are selected for measurement. Exposure calculation is based on the assumption that the reflectance of each area under consideration is similar to that of a neutral gray card. These cards typically reflect a shade of gray ranging from 12 to 18 percent, known as "middle" gray. This assumption is critical due to the varying reflectance of different objects. When photographing two cats, one dark gray and the other white, the white cat may reflect significantly more light than the grey cat. When you focus solely on the gray cat, the white cat may appear to fade away. However, if you include the white cat, the gray cat may appear black. A thorough understanding of exposure is critical for capturing accurate images. The key in the image above is to measure the amount of light reflected by a middle-gray patch, which typically reflects 12 to 18% of the incident light. The camera's exposure meter detects an object precisely and calculates the exposure to capture its true tonal value. Accurate exposure produces precise representations of both black and white patches in the image.

Overexposed images, on the other hand, occur when the exposure is calculated based on a dark area, causing the subject to appear closer to a middle gray color. This can cause darker areas to appear gray. On the other hand, images that are not properly exposed can occur when the light meter attempts to make very bright areas appear as medium gray, resulting in a decrease in exposure and making those areas too dark. To ensure precise exposure, use a gray card or another suitable alternative that reflects a consistent amount of light. When using manual or semi-automatic shooting modes, there are four ways to choose the appropriate aperture and shutter speed: aperture-priority, shutter-priority, program, and manual. When it comes to getting the perfect shot, there are several factors to consider. These include the preferred depth-of-field, motion blur preferences, and acceptable levels of noise in the image.

Aperture Priority

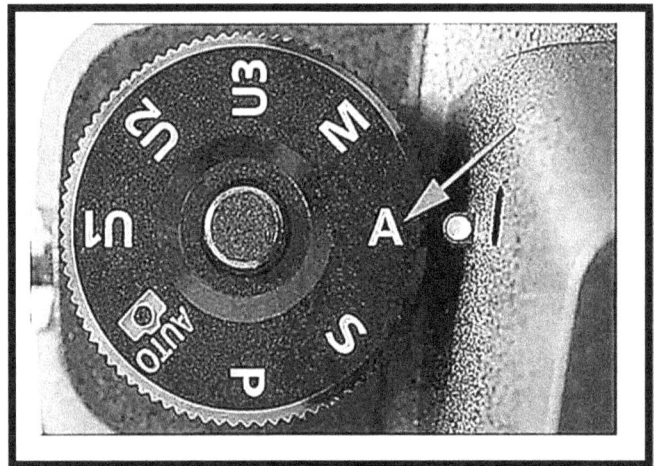

Aperture-Priority gives you precise control over the aperture setting, allowing you to create stunning images with great depth of field. With the Aperture-priority (A) mode, you can manually adjust the lens aperture while the camera handles the shutter speed, resulting in a consistent exposure with your selected ISO sensitivity. When you change the aperture, the camera smoothly adjusts the shutter speed to maintain consistent exposure while taking into account the input from the integrated light meter. This mode is especially useful for creating specific photographic effects. When it comes to close-up photography, using the smallest f-stop available (f/22) can improve depth of field. Larger f-stops, on the other hand, can help to blur the background while keeping the subject in focus. Users can also consider choosing a specific f-stop for the lens's best sharpness or striking a balance between shutter speed and image quality. For example, they can select f/2.8 for a lens with a maximum aperture of f/1.4. In addition, the Aperture-priority mode allows users to choose from a variety of shutter speeds to suit different lighting conditions.

For example, when using a telephoto lens to capture fast-paced outdoor activities like a soccer game, users can adjust the aperture to maintain the desired depth of field. This allows the camera to automatically adjust the shutter speed as the lighting changes. However, certain factors must be considered. If the aperture is set too high in comparison to the available shutter speeds, the camera may not achieve the best possible exposure. In situations with bright lighting, such as on a sunny beach or in snowy conditions, using a wide aperture like f/2.8 can result in overexposure if the camera's shutter speed isn't fast enough to handle the amount of light coming in. In low-light conditions, however, using a smaller aperture, such as f/8, may result in a slower shutter speed. This could potentially result in motion blur or camera shake. To alert users to such situations, the camera can display a blinking top-panel monochrome LCD and a shutter speed indicator in the viewfinder. This indicates that the selected aperture may cause overexposure or underexposure with the current ISO setting. Despite these limitations, aperture-priority mode remains a useful tool for photographers who want to control depth-of-field and achieve desired creative effects while maintaining consistent exposure. Aperture priority mode is highly regarded by experienced photographers, who frequently set their cameras to "A" by habit. Its exposure indicator scale, which is visible on both the control panel and the viewfinder, makes it easy to assess any potential underexposure or overexposure issues. Here is an example that shows the practical use of Aperture Priority mode in photography.

Now, we can explore different scenarios where Aperture Priority Mode is incredibly useful:

General Landscape Photography: The z8 camera is exceptional at capturing vast landscapes with intricate detail. Aperture priority mode is ideal for capturing sharpness across the landscape by increasing depth of field. This is typically accomplished by using apertures like f/11 or f/16. Photographers should use a fast shutter speed to avoid motion blur, especially when photographing distant tree branches or foliage. If you have to shoot handheld, you may need to increase the ISO slightly to ensure a fast enough shutter speed. Special Landscape Photography: In some landscape situations, aperture priority mode can result in longer shutter speeds, which are ideal for capturing the smooth motion of waterfalls. Photographers can achieve the effects they want by adjusting their cameras' f/stop and shutter speed. If you want to capture longer exposures, use neutral-density filters to control how much light enters the camera. This is a useful technique when using aperture priority mode as a starting point.

Portrait: When shooting portraits, use aperture priority mode with a medium-large aperture (f/5.6 or f/8) and a longer lens to create stunningly blurred backgrounds that draw attention to the subject's face. Larger apertures allow for selective focus, which keeps the subject's features sharp while creating a soft blur for distant elements. Using this technique and shooting from a three-quarter angle, you can create truly captivating portraits. If you want to achieve perfect focus, each lens has a specific aperture that produces the clearest and sharpest images. This sweet spot is typically a few stops below the lens's maximum aperture. Aperture priority mode allows photographers to easily select the aperture while ensuring the desired level of sharpness in their images. Macro and Close-up Photography: Macro photography requires careful f-stop selection due to the importance of depth of field. Understanding the effects of various aperture sizes can significantly improve your photography. Wider apertures draw attention to the subject, whereas smaller apertures allow you to achieve a greater depth of field. Aperture priority mode is extremely useful in these situations, especially when using cameras mounted on tripods and not having to worry about long exposure times.

Shutter Priority

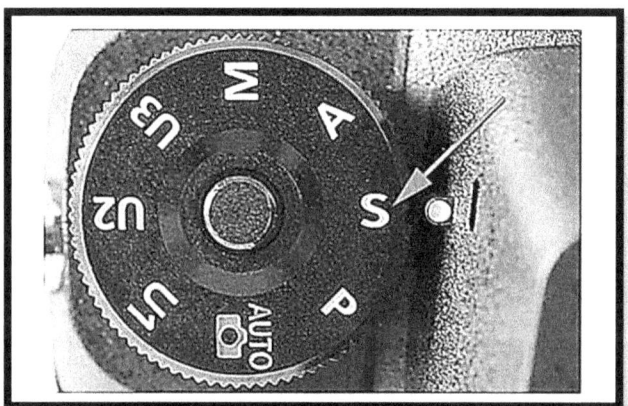

Shutter-Priority mode is a fantastic feature for photography enthusiasts who want to have more control over their camera settings. It allows you to prioritize the shutter speed while the camera automatically adjusts the aperture for optimal exposure. This is a must-have tool for capturing fast-moving objects. In shutter-priority (S) mode, the metering system determines the appropriate f/stop based on the shutter speed set by the photographer. It provides a different approach to aperture-priority mode. This mode provides precise control over the representation of motion in photographs, catering to a wide range of creative intentions. There are times when capturing fast-moving subjects is critical, necessitating the use of the highest shutter speed available. On the other hand, adding motion blur can sometimes add energy to a static photo. This can be accomplished by setting a slower shutter speed. Shutter-priority mode gives photographers complete control over their camera's ability to freeze action, allowing them to adjust it as needed for the scene. Slow shutter speeds of 1/8 second or less require extreme caution. Camera movement can cause distortion, so features like vibration reduction or a tripod can help to minimize this. Just like with aperture-priority mode, choosing a shutter speed that is either too long or too short for the right exposure can present some difficulties. When situations like this arise, you may notice that the shutter speed indicator in the viewfinder and control panel LCD starts to flicker. This is a clear indication that there might be some exposure issues to be aware of.

Now, let's see scenarios where using shutter-priority mode can be advantageous:

Eliminating Subject Motion Blur

- **Increase Shutter Speed**: To freeze motion and eliminate blur caused by moving subjects, increase the shutter speed. For fast-moving subjects, such as a motocross racer, a shutter speed of 1/200th of a second can capture the motion with minimal distortion. For even faster action, like a basketball player mid-dunk, a shutter speed of 1/1000th of a second can completely freeze the action.

Introducing Subject Motion Blur

- **Longer Shutter Speeds**: To convey a sense of motion, use a slower shutter speed. For instance, capturing flowing waterfalls with a shutter speed of one to two seconds can create a smooth, flowing effect, enhancing the dynamic quality of the image. Shutter-priority mode is ideal for controlling this effect.

Introducing Camera Motion Blur

- **Moderate Shutter Speed**: When panning with a moving subject, like relay sprinters, a moderate shutter speed (e.g., 1/60 second) can create a striking effect where the background is blurred, but the subject remains in focus. This technique enhances the sense of speed and motion in the image.

Minimizing Camera Motion Blur

- **Shutter-Priority Mode**: When photographing from a moving vehicle, such as a train or car, camera motion blur can be problematic. Adjusting the shutter speed in shutter-priority mode helps counteract the movement, resulting in sharper images. This technique ensures that your shots remain clear despite the camera's motion.

Hand-Held Landscape Photography

- **Tripod-Free Flexibility**: For landscapes, especially in windy conditions, shooting without a tripod can offer flexibility. Shutter-priority mode allows for quick adjustments to shutter speed, minimizing camera motion. Pair this with an optimized ISO setting to balance aperture and image quality, achieving a sharp and well-exposed landscape.

Concert and Stage Performance Photography

- **Lens and Shutter Speed**: Using a 70-200mm f/2.8 VR Nikkor lens with the FTZ adapter provides clarity for distant subjects. For capturing stage performances, a shutter speed of 1/180 second, combined with vibration reduction, helps prevent camera shake and ensures sharp images. This is crucial for capturing dynamic moments with minimal blur, even when shooting without a tripod.

Program Mode

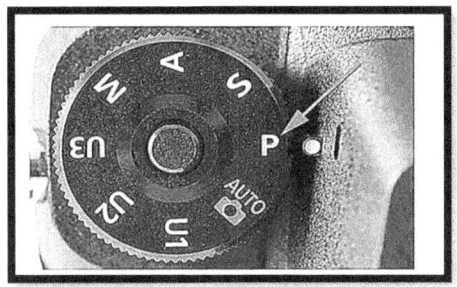

Program mode (P) utilizes the camera's advanced capabilities to automatically calculate the best aperture and shutter speed settings for any given scene. This knowledge is derived from a vast database of picture data, allowing the camera to make well-informed decisions about exposure settings. If the ISO setting doesn't give you the exposure you want, the viewfinder and control panel will let you know with blinking indicators, so you can make the necessary adjustments. This can be easily adjusted by increasing or decreasing the ISO sensitivity. Program mode provides photographers with a great deal of flexibility when it comes to adjusting exposure settings by manipulating the exposure value (EV) setting. When in Program mode, simply rotate the main command dial to access the appropriate setting. This will result in the same exposure but with a different combination of aperture and shutter speed. Nikon refers to Program Mode as a "Flexible Program," which perfectly describes its versatility. You can decrease your camera's aperture setting by rotating the main command dial to the left. For example, you can switch from f/4 to f/5.6. As a result, the camera's shutter speed will be automatically adjusted to accommodate the change. For example, it could go from 1/200th to 1/125th second. When you rotate the main command dial to the right, the aperture increases and the camera automatically adjusts the shutter speed to maintain a consistent exposure. If you see an asterisk next to the letter P in the viewfinder or monitor, it indicates that the preset program setting has been overridden. The visual cue will remain until you reset the adjustment. Even with the camera's advanced exposure calculations, there are times when photographers might want to adjust the recommended exposure settings. One technique to consider is intentionally adjusting the exposure to achieve a silhouette effect or a high-key appearance. The camera allows for these adjustments through the exposure compensation mechanism, which can be accessed by pressing a button near the shutter release. Photographers can easily adjust exposure compensation by turning the main command dial. This adjustment will remain in effect until manually reset, ensuring consistent exposure across multiple shots. In addition, the

Easy Exposure Compensation feature is easily accessible via Custom Setting b2. This allows for quick adjustments to the EV value via the main or sub-command dials, eliminating the need to press the EV button. This enhancement significantly improves user convenience, particularly when operating in Program, Aperture-priority, Shutter-priority, or Manual exposure modes. Program mode (P) is ideal for all of your shooting requirements, providing a simple solution that combines automatic exposure calculation with the ability to make some user adjustments. **Now, let's see the instances where this mode can be really helpful:**

Quick Capture

- **Program Mode for Speed**: When you're pressed for time and need to capture a moment quickly, Program mode (P mode) is ideal. This mode leverages the camera's technology to automatically select the optimal exposure settings, allowing you to snap a photo without manual adjustments. This ensures you can capture spontaneous moments with minimal effort and a good level of accuracy.

Beginner Photography

- **Ease of Use**: For photography novices, Program mode offers a user-friendly introduction to camera settings. By setting the camera to P mode, beginners can focus on composing their shots without worrying about manual exposure settings. The camera takes care of calculating the correct exposure, making it easier for newcomers to capture well-exposed images while they learn the basics of photography.

Minimal Adjustment Scenarios

- **Versatility and Simplicity**: Program mode is particularly useful in scenarios where precise adjustments to aperture and shutter speed are unnecessary. It's a versatile all-purpose setting suitable for everyday photography. While the camera handles the main exposure settings, you still have the option to make simple tweaks to adjust motion blur or depth of field if needed. This flexibility allows you to adapt to various shooting conditions without requiring extensive manual control.

Manual Exposure

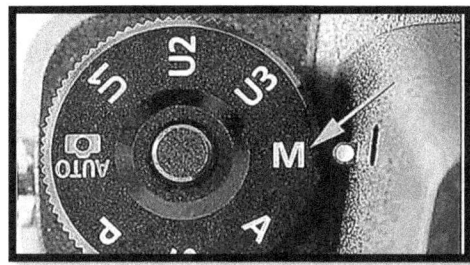

A thorough understanding of photography requires expert navigation through the various exposure modes available on a camera. These include Program mode (P) for automatic settings, Shutter-priority (S) and Aperture-priority (A) for semi-automatic control, and Manual mode (M) for full manual control. Many photographers may enjoy the precision of manually adjusting exposure, using the analog exposure scale in the viewfinder to ensure the ideal exposure. A good understanding of manual exposure can be useful in some situations. Manual adjustments are essential for capturing a striking silhouette. It enables precise control over shutter speed and aperture, allowing you to achieve effects that automated exposure modes or exposure value (EV) correction functions may not be able to provide. In a studio setting with multiple flash devices, manual adjustment is essential. The camera's metering system may not take into account external triggers that activate additional flashes, so you may need to manually adjust the aperture to ensure consistent exposure across all flashes. Although not all photographers favor manual exposure settings, it is still beneficial to have a thorough understanding of how they function. Fortunately, contemporary cameras make it much easier to manually adjust the exposure. Switching to Manual mode is simple: unlock the mode dial and turn it to the M position.

The sub-command dial and major command dial allow for simple adjustments to the aperture and shutter speed. When you partially click the shutter release or utilize the AE lock button, the viewfinder's exposure scale provides feedback, indicating any divergence from the metered exposure. It's worth noting that older lenses without a CPU processor can only be utilized in aperture-priority or manual exposure settings. However, with the Non-CPU Lens information available in the camera's Setup menu, these lenses can still be utilized efficiently. Once the camera has determined the lens's maximum aperture, changes are made via the aperture ring. When utilizing Aperture-priority mode, the camera automatically sets the shutter speed for you. In Manual mode, however, you have complete control over setting the aperture and selecting the appropriate shutter speed using the exposure scale. Manual exposure offers significant flexibility in a variety of shooting conditions, allowing photographers to painstakingly modify every step of their image-capturing process.

Below are some examples of where manual exposure is necessary:

Studio Photography

- **Full Control in a Controlled Environment**: In a studio setting, where lighting is entirely under your control, Manual mode (M) is essential. It allows you to adjust shutter speed, aperture, and ISO independently to achieve consistent exposure across all shots. Avoid using ISO Auto to maintain complete control over your exposure settings, ensuring that you achieve the desired results with every photograph.

Flash Photography

- **Precise Flash Exposure**: For using external flash units not part of the Nikon Creative Lighting System (CLS), such as studio flashes connected via PC/X flash adapters, Manual mode is crucial. It enables you to manually adjust aperture settings to match the flash exposure, ensuring that your photos are well-lit and precisely exposed according to your requirements.

Use of Hand-Held Light Meters

- **Accurate Light Measurement**: Experienced photographers can use hand-held light meters to measure both flash and continuous lighting accurately. This technique allows for precise determination of the ideal aperture for achieving perfect exposure. With this method, you can fine-tune highlights, shadows, and subject details, offering greater control over the final image's exposure.

Exposure Control

- **Creative Exposure Adjustments**: In challenging lighting conditions, such as backlighting or high-contrast scenes, Manual mode allows you to override the camera's automatic metering system. By adjusting exposure settings manually, you can create artistic effects like striking silhouettes, radiant highlights, or captivating low-key images, enabling you to explore and express your creative vision.

Aperture and Shutter Speed Control

- **Simultaneous Adjustment**: While aperture and shutter priority modes offer some control, Manual mode provides comprehensive adjustment capabilities. By setting ISO to Auto, you can maintain automatic exposure while specifying your desired aperture and shutter speed. This approach allows for precise control over both exposure parameters, making it easier to achieve the exact exposure you envision.

Long Exposures

- **Extended Exposure Capabilities**: Manual mode excels in situations requiring long exposures that semi-automatic modes might not handle effectively. By using Time or Bulb mode, you can extend exposure times up to 30 seconds or utilize the Manual mode's extended exposure function for up to 900 seconds. This feature offers precise control for capturing creative long-exposure photographs, as demonstrated in the example image showcasing the dramatic results achievable with extended exposure times.

Adjusting Exposures with ISO Settings

Understanding ISO sensitivity and how it affects image quality and exposure management will help you improve your photography skills. Photographers frequently set ISO once for a shooting session and then leave it alone. However, the ISO level can make a big difference, especially on powerful cameras like the z8. These cameras can deliver excellent results even at higher ISO settings while maintaining image quality. Adjusting the ISO provides precise control over exposure settings in various shooting modes. Manual mode allows photographers to change ISO sensitivity to add or subtract exposure adjustment. Similarly, in Program, Shutter-priority, and Aperture-priority modes, increasing the ISO produces equal exposure variations. Mastering the ISO button and the main command dial allows photographers to fine-tune exposure in precise 1/3-stop increments while maintaining their preferred aperture and shutter speed settings. When it comes to making particular exposure adjustments, ISO manipulation allows us greater versatility. For example, if the shutter priority mode suggests a shutter speed of 1/500 second at f/11 but photographers prefer 1/500 second at f/8, they can change the ISO settings to get the appropriate exposure balance. However, it is critical to exercise caution to prevent mistakenly using high ISO levels, such as ISO 6400, which might cause undesirable noise in your photographs.

The z8 camera has a wide range of ISO sensitivity settings, allowing you to capture beautiful photographs in a variety of lighting circumstances. You can change your camera's sensitivity to attain the required results by ranging from Lo 1 (equal to ISO 32) to Hi 2 (equivalent to ISO 102,400) and the normal ISO settings from ISO 64 to ISO 25,600. In addition, the camera has a wider sensitivity range, allowing you to shoot photographs at lower ISO values like Lo 1 (ISO 50 equivalent) and higher ISO values like Hi 2 (ISO 204,800 equivalent). Automatic ISO adjustment improves shooting versatility by dynamically adapting sensitivity to lighting situations depending on user-defined criteria. Auto ISO functionality offers a variety of advantages, including the ability to establish limits to avoid high ISO settings and automatically change sensitivity to ensure optimal shutter rates and reduce motion blur. However, it is vital to take caution when using Auto ISO to avoid any accidental compromises in exposure.

CHAPTER SIX

ABOUT THE CAMERA'S MID-TONE METERING

As previously stated, the most precise way to determine exposure is to put a light meter on a subject that reflects 12-18% of the incoming light. This approach ensures accurate exposure estimations. This reflecting spectrum includes topics such as a rich, medium-blue sky and lush greenery, making it ideal for calibration to ensure overall scene exposure accuracy, especially in photographs with average brightness. Nonetheless, some conditions are difficult to "meter" because they lack a mid-tone, such as bright landscapes like snow or volcanic areas. It is critical to adopt alternative approaches in such cases. One method for replacing a gray card is to utilize the palm of a human hand. However, the palm's volatility makes it less accurate when measuring. Despite this, it provides a more precise reference than a standard gray card, demanding one additional stop of exposure adjustment. To obtain suitable exposure, for example, if the meter displays 1/500th second at f/11, modify it to 1/200th second at f/11 or 1/500th second at f/8.

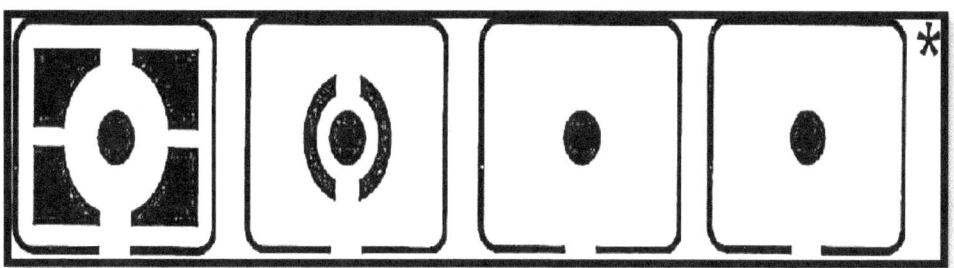

As an alternative, there are little grey card versions that fit within a camera case. Spot metering can be used to calculate exposure if the card is placed near the main subject in the frame, with its face toward the camera and evenly lighted. It's worth mentioning that many cameras are set for a slightly darker 12 percent tone, even though the average Kodak gray card reflects 18 percent of light. As a result, an additional half-stop of exposure adjustment beyond the meter reading is required to get the right exposure.

Selecting a Metering Method

The camera's exposure sensors use four metering approaches to analyze the light they receive: matrix, center-weighted, spot--, and highlight-weighted. The camera's menu lets you select your favorite mode, or you may utilize Custom Setting f2 to map the metering adjustment feature to a custom control. If you find yourself frequently switching between metering approaches, you can easily return to your preferred mode by reassigning the Fn1 or Fn2 instructions. Custom Setting f2 allows you to set these buttons for matrix-weighted, center-weighted, spot-weighted, or highlight-weighted metering. Notably, you can choose one button for center-weighted metering and another for spot metering. To ensure smooth transitions between these modes, the metering mode switch can also be set to Matrix. The viewfinder's signals, which are symbolically represented for each metering mode, aid in remembering which one was selected. Your camera can compute the exposure by evaluating the light that enters the lens and passes through to the sensor. The sensor's light detection range at ISO 100 is -3 to +17 EV, corresponding to exposure times ranging from eight minutes at f/16 to 1/1000 second at f/16. Practically, there is a wide range of light conditions: 0 EV during a full moon night and roughly 16 EV for the brightest daytime scenarios, such as snowfall in direct sunlight. Despite this large range, your camera can collect photons in an extremely wide EV range—two stops darker than full moonlight and one stop brighter than snow during the day. However, the camera's dynamic range—a measure of its capacity to preserve image detail—is lower than its detection range for bright tones. It is critical to recognize that, while the sensor has a wide tonal range for detection, its dynamic range—the number of tones it can properly record in the final image—is relatively limited. This limitation underscores how important it is to learn and use metering settings intelligently to get the best exposure possible under various lighting conditions.

Using Matrix Metering

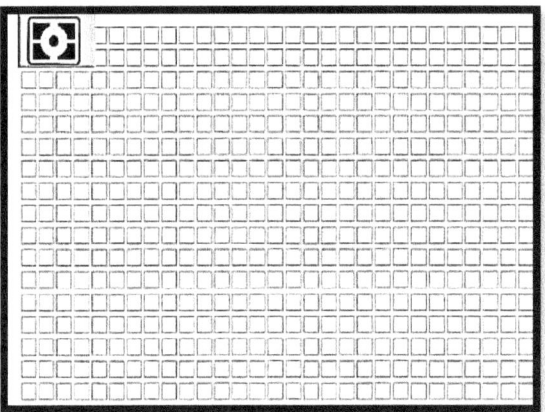

When in matrix metering mode, your camera employs an innovative algorithm to compare the brightness levels registered in different zones of the frame to the light that strikes the sensor during the incident. When matrix metering is enabled, a symbol is normally displayed in the top left corner of the screen. You can see it simply holding down the DISP button until it appears. The camera automatically recognizes the type of scenario you're shooting by examining these zones and accessing a big photo library of over 30,000 images. For example, if the top area of an image is substantially darker than the bottom, the algorithm may interpret it as a landscape scene with a prominent sky. On the other hand, if you're shooting a portrait, it may prioritize exposure for the human subject if it detects skin tones in a brighter region in the center of the frame. Matrix metering is particularly effective in circumstances involving a variety of objects and illumination due to its adaptability. Matrix metering is effective in well-lit, moderately toned environments with human figures; nevertheless, in cloudy or low-light conditions, it may result in underexposed photographs. However, the setting is usually reliable and only requires a small amount of exposure adjustment, particularly in circumstances where you have bright backdrops or snow-covered landscapes for your pictures.

Furthermore, contemporary exposure meters include further data to intelligently adjust exposure settings beyond basic luminance calculations:

1. **Patterns**:
   - **Exposure Detection**: The camera analyzes patterns across the sensor by comparing database-level similarities and pixel-level differences. It prioritizes highlight preservation, especially in high-contrast situations, recognizing that features in shadows are often retrievable, particularly when shooting in RAW format.

2. **Colors**:
   - **Color-Based Exposure Adjustment**: The camera uses color detection to refine its exposure measurements. It identifies specific colors—such as green for vegetation, skin tones for human subjects, and blue for the sky—to adjust exposure settings and ensure accurate color reproduction.

3. **Autofocus Region**:
   - **In-Focus Area Prioritization**: The camera adjusts the exposure based on the autofocus region, whether the subject is manually selected by the user or automatically chosen by the camera's autofocus system. It assumes that the focus area is accurately represented and adjusts exposure accordingly to maintain clarity and detail.

4. **Aspect Ratio and Focal Length**:
   - **Scene Type Adjustment**: The camera utilizes data from Z-mount lenses, including focal length and distance, to tailor exposure settings based on the scene type. For instance, it adjusts exposure differently for landscape shots with a wide-angle lens compared to portrait shots with a telephoto lens, optimizing the settings for each specific scenario.

Matrix metering is suitable for a wide range of general themes due to its analytical abilities and precise subject matter estimates. It can discern between scenes with low and high contrast, and it frequently underexposes slightly in high-contrast scenarios to preserve highlight detail. However, when using powerful filters like split-color, polarizing, graded neutral-density, or very dark filters, it is recommended to use center-weighted metering. These filters have the potential to provide incorrect exposures by interfering with the relationships between different frame sections used in matrix metering calculations. A polarizing filter, for example, can drastically darken the sky, impairing the camera's ability to distinguish landscape images.

Center-Weighted Metering

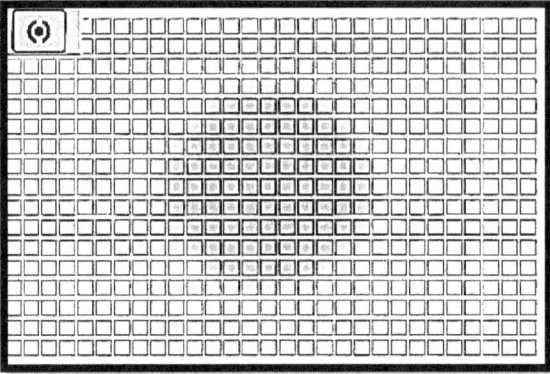

When utilizing center-weighted metering, the camera calculates exposure by prioritizing a 12mm zone in the center of the image. This strategy outperformed averaging, which simply totaled up the brightness for the entire frame. It comes before more advanced metering approaches. Center-weighted metering, unlike matrix metering, does not require advanced scene analysis. Instead, it assumes that the major topic is typically centered in most photographs and considers the overall brightness of the frame while focusing more on the central region. The 12mm center region accounts for roughly 75% of the exposure calculation, with the remaining 25% influenced by the frame's contents. For example, if the camera determines that the core area requires an exposure of f/4 at 1/250 second, it will prioritize the center area and compute a final exposure of roughly f/5.6 at 1/250 second, but the outlying areas require an exposure of f/16 at 1/250 second. A mid-tone topic in the middle is required for effective usage of center-weighted metering. However, if there are extensive areas of extreme brightness or blackness around the focus point, exposure may not be the ideal choice. Despite this disadvantage, center-weighted metering is quite useful for photographing close-ups or portraits of things like flowers. When utilizing center-weighted metering, you can either utilize the conventional 12mm circle or select "Average," which considers the entire frame and calculates exposure using average values. Because of its versatility, you can adjust the metering mode to suit diverse objects and shooting scenarios.

Spot Metering

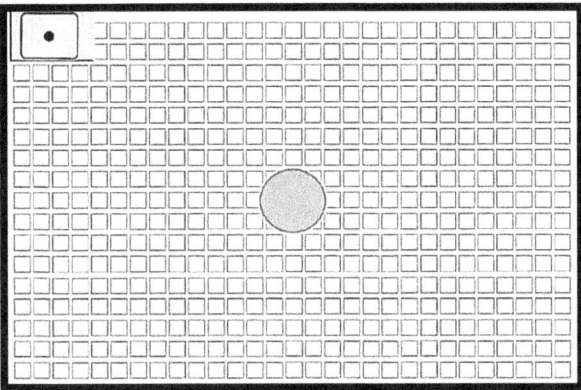

Spot metering is often the option of choice for photographers with expertise with handheld light meters, particularly those who are used to measuring highlights and shadows independently. Spot metering makes it possible to measure light reflected from certain areas of a subject precisely, regardless of whether those areas are bright, midtone, dark, or a mix of these. The viewfinder's viewing area is limited to a tiny 4mm area in this mode, making up just 1.5% of the screen. It is critical to understand that this circle is larger than the focus point itself, even if it is centered on the active focus point (which may or may not be the one depicted in the figure). As a result, evaluating exposure is not restricted to the indicators associated with the active focal point. The only technique that allows for precise exposure measurement placement within the frame is spot metering. Spot metering is useful for determining exposure for certain sections of a frame, especially when such regions are located in the frame's center. If the subject is off-center, you must set the exposure by partially pressing the shutter release button or clicking the center of the sub-selector after obtaining a meter reading with the appropriate focus point. This option works best when the backdrop is noticeably lighter or darker than the subject.

Extremely bright or dark tonality while metering an area might lead to overexposure or underexposure, respectively, requiring a manual override to get more accurate readings. Spot metering, however, may provide acceptable results when used to measure a tiny mid-tone subject against a wall of indigo blue or big white clouds. Spot metering benefits considerably from your participation in choosing the metering position, in contrast to the matrix and center-weighted metering, which provide little flexibility and mostly depend on modifications to settings like Custom Setting b4: Fine-Tune Optimal Exposure and exposure compensation.

There are many things to factor in when using this mode:

Changing the Spot

- **AF-Area Mode Selection**: To alter the AF spot, you need to use an AF-area mode that allows for changing the AF point. The exception is auto-area autofocus (AF), which always uses the center focus point as the metering spot and does not permit adjustments.

Choosing an Appropriate AF-Area Mode

- **i Menu Customization**: The i menu provides options to select different focus areas depending on the chosen focus mode. This allows you to tailor the autofocus point to match your shooting requirements.

Wrap Around

- **Adjusting Metering and AF Points**: You can rotate the metering area and adjust the AF point on the display using the directional controls on the multi-selector or sub-selector. This enables precise placement of the AF point for optimal focus and exposure.

Auto-Area AF

- **Spot Metering Integration**: While spot metering is generally more effective when not using auto-area AF, it can still be utilized in this mode with some limitations. Auto-area AF primarily relies on the central focus point, offering less flexibility in choosing the specific metering area.

It should be noted that the spot metering point changes along with the focus point. Additionally, when using Dynamic-area AF for continuous focusing, the camera may change the focus point it originally chose and concentrate on nearby spots, moving the metering area accordingly.

Highlight Weighted Metering

Similar to matrix metering, the exposure system looks at the whole scene while in highlight-weighted metering mode. This mode functions independently of spot metering, even though it shares the Spot emblem with an asterisk. Rather, the twin

Expeed 6 processors locate the parts in your picture that are highlighted and then modify exposure in those areas to avoid overexposure. The exposure estimate assigns less weight to places that are not stated. Highlight-weighted metering works particularly well in scenes with highlights scattered throughout the frame. For example, when photographing spotlit artists on stage at a performance, the camera may correctly compute exposure by considering the performers individually while disregarding the poorly lit environment. Spot metering can also be utilized by placing the metering spot on the performer's face or shirt; however, highlight-weighted metering is more automatic and relies solely on highlights to calculate exposure. Highlight-weighted metering's efficiency is determined by the precision with which the spot region is positioned and the system's ability to identify the subject from the backdrop. For example, highlight-weighted metering guarantees that actors are adequately exposed during a theatrical performance, even when the lighting changes. Regardless of the metering technique employed, ensuring exposure becomes critical once shutter speed, aperture, and ISO settings are set to your taste. This capability allows you to recompose a shot before it is taken. When using the AE-L/AF-L setup, the sub-selector center button ensures exposure and autofocus by default. Nevertheless, you may designate a different control—like the AF-ON button—for this feature by going to Custom Setting f2: Custom Controls. The given control can be used as either an AE Lock Only or an AE/AF lock. The latter is especially useful when employing back-button focus. Using the same custom option, you can also create a Shutter Speed and Aperture Lock button that employs aperture priority to lock the aperture or shutter speed. This ensures consistency and control over exposure settings, enhancing your ability to capture exact images.

Handling Noise

Though it is sometimes used purposely as a specific effect, visual image noise—defined by its grainy, random appearance—is frequently seen as undesirable since it adds unwanted texture and diminishes picture detail. Long exposure times and high ISO settings are the primary culprits of this noise. As the ISO level is increased, the camera produces more high ISO noise. This occurs when the camera amplifies the basic signal that was originally recorded at lower ISO levels (for example, ISO 64 or ISO 100 on the Z8). The addition of a dual gain signal amplifier to cameras is a significant advancement in technology since it improves performance at higher ISO settings. Interestingly, it maintains image quality and provides great contrast at sub-base ISO levels as low as Lo 1. Even at ISO 800 and higher, noise may still be captured in photographs; however, noise starts to show about ISO 1600 and is often quite obvious at ISO 6400. Noise may become a considerable annoyance at ISO 25,800 and above, however, ISO 25,600 can still provide some good shots of scenes with low contrast.

Nikon designates its higher ISO 25,600 levels as Hi 0.3 through Hi 2 and advises against using them unless necessary. Pictures taken at this high resolution usually have more noise and contrast. The amplification required to increase the sensitivity of the sensor is the reason for the high ISO noise. Increased ISOs bring out features in poorly lit situations, but they also cause noise by amplifying non-signal information. The Photo Shooting menu's High ISO NR (Noise Reduction) option allows you to disable the function completely or set it to High, Normal, or Low. Remember that noise reduction might result in a softer, pixelated look and a decrease in picture quality. You may turn this function off if you would rather have greater information at the risk of some noise. Longer exposure durations increase the amount of photons that reach the sensor and enhance the camera's capacity to take pictures in low light. However, they also contribute to noise. Longer exposure lengths, on the other hand, increase the likelihood of random noise since the sensor may mistake rising temperatures for heat rather than light. CMOS sensors, like those used in the Z8, are particularly susceptible to fixed-pattern noise, a type of noise induced by variances between individual amplifiers and A/D converters. Nikon worked hard to reduce noise in the camera from every perspective. To further minimize noise, use the Long Exposure Noise Reduction option in the Photo Shooting menu. This tool detects and removes noisy pixels by comparing a second, empty exposure to the original image. Nonetheless, the image may lose some detail as a result of this process. Furthermore, noise reduction can be applied in post-processing with RAW converters or Photoshop software. Noise from processed images can also be successfully eliminated using specialized software like Noise Ninja. It is important to apply noise reduction with caution to avoid losing too much visual detail.

CHAPTER SEVEN

ABOUT THE Z8 BRACKETING

Bracketing is a technique in which multiple consecutive exposures are taken with different settings to increase the likelihood of obtaining perfectly correct exposures. Beyond simple exposure adjustments, bracketing can also be used to create a series of photographs with marginally different exposures or white balances to select the "best" picture from an artistic standpoint. Bracketing, for example, can produce three different exposures: normal for a backlit subject, underexposed for a silhouette effect, and overexposed for an additional visual dimension. The Z8 can bracket exposures, white balance, and active D-lighting. Auto exposure bracketing (AEB) is most commonly utilized for critical color accuracy, while white balance (WB) bracketing is used on occasion. When the AEB is activated, the camera takes a series of consecutive photographs, the first of which is taken at the preset "correct" exposure, followed by photographs with decreasing exposure, and finally shots with exposure rising by the appropriate increment of +3/-3 stops. Using the Shutter Priority (S) or Aperture Priority (A) modes, bracketed exposures are created by adjusting the aperture or shutter speed.

Although setting up AEB settings may appear difficult, it may be made easier by doing the following steps:

1. Choose the bracketing type: Open the Photo Shooting menu, select Auto Bracketing, and then Auto Bracketing Set to select the proper bracketing type. The offered choices include ADL bracketing, flash only, white balance alone, auto exposure with flash, and flash only.
Custom Setting e6 allows you to select between flash and shutter speed, aperture and flash and shutter speed, flash and aperture, or flash just when modifying the bracketing process configuration in Manual exposure mode. In manual exposure mode, ADL and white balance bracketing are not available.
2. Choose the bracketing order: Navigate to Custom Setting e7 and then select from; MTR > Under > Over or Under > MTR > Over.
3. Choose the number of bracketed exposures: To determine the number of bracketed exposures, select Number of Shots from the Auto Bracketing option. To decide how many overexposed or underexposed photographs to include in the sequence, utilize the multi-selector buttons or the touch screen.

4. Choose the bracket increment: Using the Increment option, choose 1/3, 2/3, 1, 2, or 3 EV increments to determine the exposure increment. Keep in mind that choosing 2 or 3 EV increments limits the number of images in the bracketed collection to 5.

5. In Single-frame mode, press the shutter release button the designated number of times for each exposure in your bracketed burst. The camera adjusts exposure, flash level, and white balance for each image in the sequence specified in Custom Setting e7, based on the chosen bracketing "program."

6. Deactivate bracketing: To do so, return to the Auto Bracketing entry and set the Number of Shots to zero after the bracketing procedure is complete. Because the setting is active even after turning the camera on and off again, this prevents the BKT indicator from displaying.

Note: Capturing a succession of bracketed exposures is simple if the type of bracketing is defined. When bracketing is enabled, simply click the Bracketing Burst sign to begin setting the exposure. Each touch of the shutter release button records the complete set. (Custom setting f2 lets you map the Bracketing Burst behavior to a button).

White Balance Bracketing

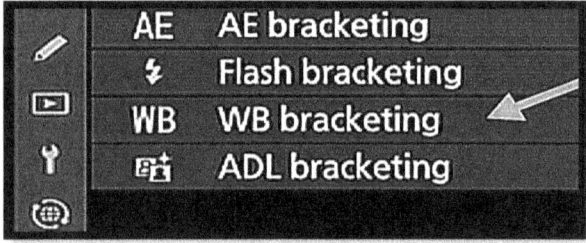

Regardless of the mode selection (JPEG, RAW, or RAW+JPEG), the camera simplifies the process when white balance bracketing is enabled by taking just one RAW exposure at first. The camera then produces JPEG files at every designated white balance level. With only one click, this approach provides two or three JPEG files of the necessary quality level, thereby reducing the number of photographs that must be taken. Multiple RAW shots are not necessary since the camera automatically creates JPEG files at the desired white balance settings, even though RAW files include all the information received during exposure. When the camera is configured to shoot in JPEG-only mode, the RAW data is deleted after the first RAW exposure is converted into a JPEG format using the chosen parameters. However, when in RAW mode, the camera saves the RAW data as a NEF file and generates a Basic JPEG version that is included as a thumbnail in the RAW file. It's worth noting that the RAW file is only accessible when imported into an image editing tool; while viewing photos on the camera's LCD panel, you'll see the embedded JPEG thumbnail. When saving in RAW+JPEG format, a separate JPEG file with the specified quality level (Fine, Normal, or Basic) is created; otherwise, the embedded JPEG image is included in the NEF RAW file. Unlike exposure bracketing, which adjusts JPEG files by f-stops, white balance bracketing modifies the color temperature using micro reciprocal degrees, or mireds. Every image in the bracket set is subjected to a 5 mired color temperature change, which modifies the amber-blue spectrum but does not affect the green-magenta color bias.

To activate white balance bracketing, do the following actions:

1. Configure Image Quality: Ensure that JPEG-only is selected under the Image Quality option in the Photo Shooting menu.
2. Choose WB Bracketing: Select WB Bracketing as your bracketing configuration by selecting it from the Auto Bracketing option in the Photo Shooting menu.
3. Select Number of Shots: After picking WB Bracketing, go to Number of Shots and input the appropriate number of bracketed exposures. There are two choices available to you:
- To ensure an equitable distribution of shots on both sides of the zero point on the amber-blue scale, use the right directional button to choose between zero and nine shots. One neutral shot and two each with biases of five and ten mireds in the amber and blue directions, respectively, would result from choosing five shots.
- Select from two or three photographs with applied amber (A) or blue (B) biases by using the left directional button. If B3 were chosen, for example, biases of 5, 10, and 15 mireds would only be in the blue direction.

ADL Bracketing

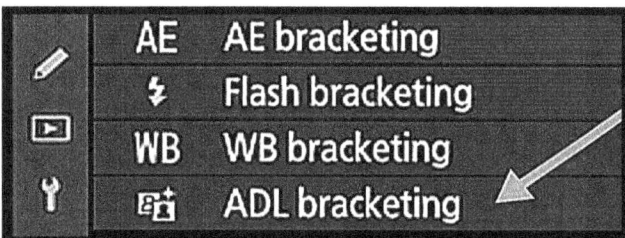

To activate Active D-Lighting bracketing, go to the Photo Shooting menu and select Auto Bracketing Set. The number of shots and the Active D-Lighting parameters are set here. Similar to exposure bracketing, if you've assigned a Bracketing Burst button, you can fire off a burst of images with a single press of the shutter release button.

 Below is a summary of the available options:

0 Shots:

- **Disable Active D-Lighting Bracketing**: This setting completely turns off Active D-Lighting bracketing. However, if enabled in the Shooting menu, basic Active D-Lighting with settings ranging from Auto to Low may still be applied to every photo.

2 Shots:

- **Capture Two Images**: Take two photos: the first one with Active D-Lighting off (serving as the control) and the second with the chosen ADL setting applied. To adjust the ADL setting, access the Amount box and select from the following options:
    - Off/Auto
    - Off/Extra High
    - Off/High
    - Off/Normal
    - Off/Low

3-5 Shots:

- **Choose the Number of Shots**: Select between three, four, or five shots with varying ADL settings:
    - **For 3 Shots**: Capture with ADL settings set to Low, Normal, and Off.
    - **For 4 Shots**: Capture with ADL settings set to Off, Low, Normal, and High.
    - **For 5 Shots**: Capture with ADL settings set to Off, Low, Normal, High, and Extra High.
- **Note**: The Amount box for these pictures does not allow changing the ADL settings for the different shots.

Disabling ADL Bracketing

- **Turn off When Not in Use**: To disable ADL bracketing when it's not needed, follow the same procedure used for WB, exposure, and flash bracketing. ADL bracketing remains enabled by default until specifically turned off, which helps avoid unexpected impacts on your photographs and ensures consistent results.

CHAPTER EIGHT

WORKING WITH HDR

Go to the Auto Bracketing Set option under the Photo Shooting menu to turn on Active D-Lighting bracketing. The number of shots and the Active D-Lighting parameters for each shot may be adjusted here. If you've designated a Bracketing Burst button for simplicity of use, you may initiate a quick series of images with a single push of the shutter release button, much like exposure bracketing.

Now let's see the options available:

1. **0 Shots**:
   - **Disable Active D-Lighting Bracketing**: Selecting this option turns off Active D-Lighting bracketing completely. This mode only disables bracketing; however, if basic Active D-Lighting is enabled in the Shooting menu, the chosen ADL level (Auto, Extra High, High, Normal, or Low) will still be applied to every shot.

2. **2 Shots**:
   - **Two Successive Photos**: This setting captures two photos: the first with the selected ADL setting, and the second as a reference shot with ADL turned off (control shot). Configure this by selecting one of the following options in the Amount box:
     - **Off/Auto**: Applies Auto ADL to one shot and no ADL to the other.
     - **Off/Extra High**
     - **Off/High**
     - **Off/Normal**
     - **Off/Low**

3. **3–5 Shots**:
   - **Multiple Shots**: Choose to capture three, four, or five shots. In each set, one shot will have ADL turned off, and the remaining shots will use the ADL settings specified in the Amount area. After capturing, the ADL settings for these shots remain fixed and cannot be changed in the Amount box:
     - **For 3 Shots**: Take pictures with ADL settings set to Low, Normal, and Off.
     - **For 4 Shots**: Take pictures with ADL settings set to Off, Low, Normal, and High.
     - **For 5 Shots**: Take pictures with ADL settings set to Off, Low, Normal, High, and Extra High.

Auto-HDR

Assume you're attempting to portray the contrast between the bright light flooding in from outside the window and the dim mood of a poorly lit room. It is challenging to achieve the optimal exposure for both components. The outer scene requires settings around f/11 at 1/400 second, whilst the interior may require 1/60 second at f/2.8 and ISO 200. Because of this massive variance in exposure levels, which frequently exceeds the dynamic range capabilities of even the most powerful digital cameras, such as the z8, which has an estimated dynamic range of 7 f-stops or 7 EV steps. However, given current restrictions, future improvements should result in sensors with significantly greater dynamic ranges—possibly far closer than we believe. However, until then, it is critical to become adept in cutting-edge techniques such as Active D-lighting and HDR (High Dynamic Range) photography. These strategies allow photographers to efficiently capture situations with significant contrast. For example, the z8 allows you to create HDR exposures directly in the camera. Alternatively, you can use the more typical way of shooting individual bracketed exposures and combining them using post-processing tools like Adobe's Merge to HDR feature or Photomatix.

This is a thorough rundown on how to use HDR:

- **In-camera HDR**: Without the need for additional software, combine many exposures into a single high dynamic range picture directly from the camera by using the z8's integrated HDR features.
- **Traditional HDR Bracketing**: To fully capture the dynamic range of the scene, take a series of bracketed exposures at different settings. For best effects, later combine these exposures using specialized HDR software.

With the use of these techniques, photographers may get around restrictions on dynamic range and create breathtaking shots that accurately capture the scene's depth and contrast, giving them the greatest amount of artistic freedom and visual impact. Despite its simplicity and lack of customization, the in-camera high dynamic range (HDR) tool performs admirably in boosting images with a wide dynamic range. With a three-stop/EV exposure differential option comparable to bracketed exposures, it is similar to manual HDR approaches, even though it just merges two exposures into a single HDR image. Because digital sensors have a limited dynamic range, it is difficult to obtain the desired balance of highlight and shadow detail in a single image. However, the camera's Auto HDR feature provides an answer by blending two exposures into one in a smooth manner, extending the range of tones that can be captured. Consider combining two separate photographs, one with an underexposure and one with an overexposure. The resulting HDR image improves the visual experience by displaying a considerably wider tonal range. Follow these instructions to use the HDR features. However, it should be noted that it is not available while using bracketing, multiple exposures, or time-lapse photography, nor is it compatible with RAW or RAW+JPEG styles of photography.

Access the Menu: Pick the MENU button (a camera symbol will appear) to open the Photo Shooting menu.

HDR Settings: To access the four options—HDR Mode, Exposure Differential, Smoothing, and Save Individual Images—scroll down to HDR and hit the multi-selector button on the right.

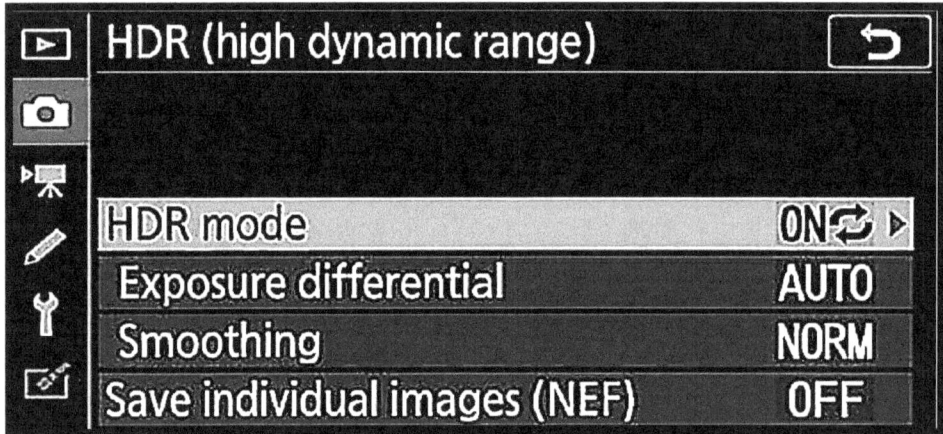

Activate HDR: Pick HDR Mode, then click on (single photo) or On (series) to take one or more HDR pictures. Click OK to confirm.

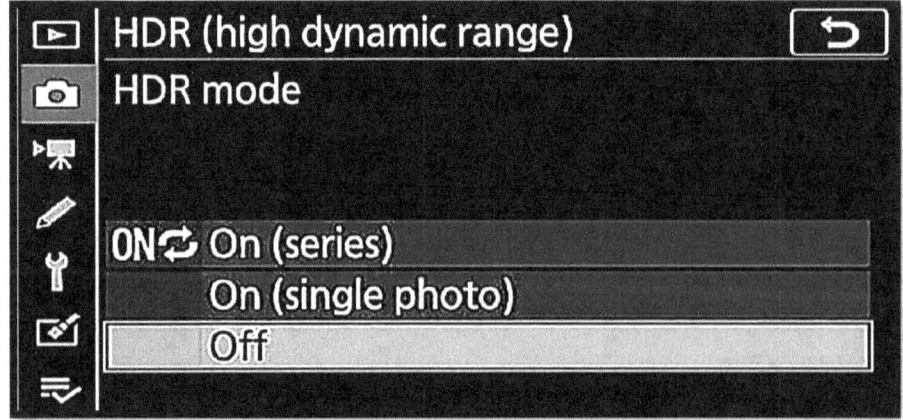

73

Adjust Exposure Differential: The contrast ratio between exposures may be set by picking the "Exposure Differential" option, which has a range of Auto to 3 EVs. Pick OK to verify your choice.

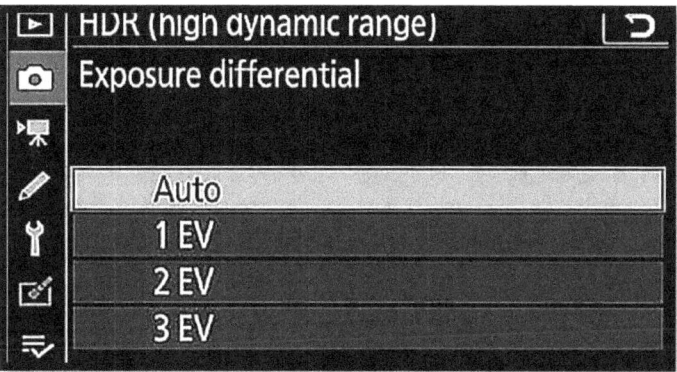

Smoothing Option: Pick Smoothing to lessen haloing around picture areas. To adjust the effect, pick Normal, Low, or High smoothing levels.

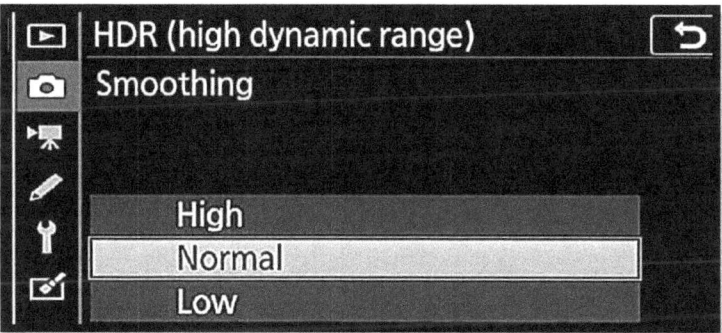

Save Single Images (Optional): To save individual RAW versions of taken photos for computer post-processing, enable **Save Individual Images** (NEF).

Set Aperture-Priority Mode: Ensure that your camera is in Aperture-Priority mode so you may vary the f-stop to manage exposure while keeping a constant depth-of-field.

Take the Shot: Although handheld HDR photography is possible, utilizing a tripod to reduce camera movement yields the best results. The camera's alignment attempts might cause even little movement to result in cropping at the picture edges. Therefore, using a tripod is advised, particularly with Auto HDR.

Bracketing and Merge to HDR

Manual HDR photography can still be done by bypassing your camera's HDR function. To take individual photographs, however, you can utilize either manual or automated bracketing approaches. Merge to HDR Pro captures several photographs, some of which are used as exposure changes for highlights, midtones, and shadows. It is up to you to determine how many images to include. The well-exposed portions from each version are then combined using the Merge to HDR Pro command, resulting in a single HDR image. Aside from exposure, the photos should be as close as possible.

As such, it is best to utilize a remote release device, such as the MC-DC2, to record each exposure at the same time, and to set the camera on a tripod. Follow the steps below:

Camera Setup:
- **Mounting**: Securely mount the camera to a tripod to ensure stability and avoid any camera shake during the bracketed exposures.

Bracketed Burst Settings:
- **Configure Bracketing**: Set the camera to take bracketed bursts with intervals of two or three EVs (exposure values) to capture a range of exposures for HDR processing.

Aperture Selection:
- **Choose Aperture**: Select an aperture that provides precise exposure for the bracketed series. Set the camera to aperture-priority mode to control the depth of field and exposure settings.

Manual Focus:
- **Avoid Focus Shifts**: Switch the camera to manual focus mode to prevent any focus inconsistencies between the bracketed shots. Carefully adjust the focus on the subject to ensure consistency across all images.

RAW Exposures:
- **Capture in RAW**: Opt to shoot in RAW format to retain the maximum range of tones and details, which is crucial for effective HDR processing.

Capture Bracketed Exposures:
- **Take Photos**: Capture the series of bracketed exposures by either using a remote shutter release, gently pressing the shutter button, or utilizing the self-timer feature to avoid camera shake.

Merge to HDR Pro:
- **Follow Instructions**: After capturing the bracketed exposures, proceed with the Merge to HDR Pro function in your photo editing software. Follow the on-screen instructions to combine the bracketed images into a single HDR photograph, adjusting settings as needed to achieve the desired result.

CHAPTER NINE

NIKON WHITE BALANCE

This function is used to maintain the proper color temperature when taking images. It neutralizes or balances the overall color temperature by employing the color associated with it in the frame. For example, when incandescent lighting is employed, the lack of blue might result in items seeming greenish-yellow. Adding a little blue to a photograph can make the colors appear more coordinated and harmonious. Similarly, if it's foggy or cloudy outside, the light in the interior may cast the scene in a cold blue hue. If you do not repair these alterations, your images may take on a blue hue. However, your camera's white balance (WB) feature detects the cool color temperature and compensates for it by adding warmth, usually through red tones. On a foggy day, a regular camera's WB setting may appear to be approximately 6000K. To comprehend white balance, you must first recognize that light comes in a variety of colors, ranging from cool to warm. By considering how the light source works, photographers may configure their cameras to use available light in a fair, accurate, and helpful manner. Furthermore, photographers can adjust the white balance settings to give their images specific color casts. You can adjust your camera's white balance manually in the Shooting Menu or by pressing a dedicated WB button. The following section will go into greater detail about each of these techniques, providing you with detailed instructions on how to make exact white balance alterations.

Locating the Buttons and Controls used for White Balance Adjustment

Here, we will go over how to set your camera's white balance (WB) settings. It is important to learn how to use the different buttons and settings that affect WB.

These include the Control panel, the Main and Sub-command knobs, and the WB button.

White Balance Button:
- **Function**: This button is crucial for adjusting white balance. Pressing it brings up a menu or interface where you can change your camera's white balance settings. It's the primary method for accessing and modifying white balance settings directly.

Sub-command Dial:

- **Function**: Located near the White Balance button, the Sub-command dial is used for switching between different white balance options or fine-tuning the selected setting. It allows for quick and precise adjustments to white balance settings.

Main Command Dial:
- **Function**: While primarily used for adjusting exposure, aperture, and shutter speed, the Main Command Dial can also be used to fine-tune white balance settings. It helps in making broader adjustments or navigating through white balance options when combined with other settings.

Control Panel:
- **Function**: The Control Panel displays key settings and information, including the current white balance mode or preset. It provides a visual reference for quickly checking and adjusting the white balance settings as needed.

Using the WB Button to Set the White Balance Manually

You can choose to change the white balance (WB) settings by hand if you want to. Here is a step-by-step guide on how to choose a white balance type by hand using the WB button, the Main command key, the Control panel, or the Information display:

Press the WB Button:
- **Action**: Locate and press the White Balance (WB) button on the top of your camera. This initiates the process of manually selecting the white balance settings.

Turn the Main Command Dial:
- **Action**: After pressing the WB button, use the Main Command Dial on the back of the camera to cycle through the white balance options. As you turn the dial, the available white balance settings will be displayed on both the Information Display and the Control Screen.

Using the Information Display to Navigate:
- **Action**: If necessary, press the "Info" button to view the white balance settings on the Information Display. The display will update with each turn of the Main Command Dial, showing different white balance options. If the white balance type selected has subtypes (like AUTO1), you can use the front Sub-command Dial to navigate these subtypes.

Selection Process:
- **Action**: During the selection process, the front Sub-command Dial is not used for changing the main white balance setting but may be used if subtypes are

available. If there are no subtypes, the top line of the screen showing the white balance type (e.g., "Auto White Balance") will remain blank.

You can directly change your camera's white balance settings to get the color balance you want for your photos by following these steps and using the options that are given.

Here are all the specifics and settings you need to change your camera's white balance:

Set the auto white balance to between 3500K and 8000K:

There are icons like "A" on the Control panel and "Auto" (AUTO0, AUTO1, or AUTO2) on the Information display and camera options when this mode is selected.

- **AUTO0:** Changes to cooler colors by adding less warm colors.
- **AUTO1**: Most shooters like this setting because it sets the white balance to colors that look good with the subject.
- **AUTO2**: Keeps a warm atmosphere and makes pictures that are a little warmer than normal, which many users prefer.
- - These Auto modes work with Nikkor lenses that are G, E, or D.

Natural Light Auto (4500–8000K):

- This mode makes the colors in the picture more like how people see them.
- It's like AUTO1 Normal, but it only lets you make small changes. It blends well with natural light, making it good for nature photographers.

3000K incandescent light: Great for getting true colors when using older electric light sources.

Fluorescent (2700K to 7200K): Has seven subtypes for different fluorescent lamps, from sodium-vapor (2700K) to high-temperature mercury-vapor (7200K).

Direct sunlight (5200K): Made to take pictures of things in full sunlight.

Flash (5400K): Ensure that the colors match up consistently with Nikon Speedlights.

Cloudy (6000K): Warms up pictures when it's cloudy outside.

Shade (8000K): Balances out the strong blue tint that comes from taking pictures of things in the shade with a blue sky in the background.

K (Manual Color Temperature) (2500K–10,000K): The color temperature can be chosen precisely to fit the lighting conditions.

PRE (Preset Manual):

- A white or gray card is used to check the white balance with the current light source.
- It saves this figure (d-1 to d-6) so it can be used again in the same lighting conditions.

Using the Shooting Menu(s) to Set the White Balance Manually

To finish this process, choose the right white balance setting from either the Photo Shooting Menu or the Movie Shooting Menu. The image below shows the Photo Shooting Menu, but the steps are the same for the Movie Shooting Menu as well.

To choose a white balance setting, do the following:

1. Select **White Balance** from the Photo Shooting menu. After that, move your mouse to the right.
2. As soon as you select one of the standard options, such as Flash, slide the mouse further to the right.
3. If you do not wish to modify the White Balance option, click OK without changing the little square from its original position.

Using the WB Button to Manually Select the Color Temperature

Note: The K option on the Control screen gives you options because it lets you choose a White Balance (WB) number by hand from 2500K to 10,000K. You can use the settings on the outside of the camera to set the Kelvin (K) White Balance number to the level you want.

Do these things:

1. To access the K symbol on the Control panel or Information screen, first press the WB button. Next, spin the Main Command Dial on the rear. If you wish to see the WB numbers on the information display, then turn it on by pushing the info button, and then hold down the WB button.
2. Hold down the WB button and use the front Sub-command switch to set the White Balance Kelvin temperature to any number between 2500K and 10,000K.

Manually Selecting the Color Temperature with the Shooting Menu

Through the Shooting Menu, which can be found in both the photo and video shooting menus, you can change the color temperature by hand. The Photo Shooting Menu screens let you reach the custom color temperature setting, which is a useful tool.

To set a particular Kelvin (K) White Balance setting, do the following:

1. **Navigate to White Balance Settings**:
   - **Action**: Access the Photo Shooting Menu and select **White Balance**. Move to the right to proceed.
2. **Select Color Temperature**:

- o **Action**: Continue moving to the right until you reach **Color Temperature** in the white balance settings.
3. **Adjust Color Temperature**:
   - o **Action**: Use the selection pad or touch the up-and-down arrows to scroll through color temperature options. The range available is from **2500K to 10000K**. When you select a color temperature, a large yellow square will appear on the screen next to **Pick Color Temp**. This screen is split into two sections: one for selecting the color temperature and one for fine-tuning. Scroll to the right to move the yellow triangle to the fine-tuning area.
4. **Fine-Tune the Color Temperature**:
   - o **Action**: Adjust the color temperature in 0.25 steps to either add greener (G) or magenta (M). Use the Multi-selection pad to move the slider up for more green (G0 to G6) or down for more magenta (M0 to M6).
5. **Confirm Your Selection**:
   - o **Action**: Press the **OK** button to finalize and apply your chosen color temperature setting.

Note: The white balance setting will remain consistent across all photos until you decide to change it. This ensures uniformity in white balance, which is particularly useful for maintaining consistency in studio photography or product shots.

Using the White Balance vis-à-vis using the Live View Photography Mode

When you are taking pictures in Live View mode, you can choose and tweak the white balance settings.

To start taking pictures in Live View, move the Live View button up. Do these things once you're in Live View mode:
1. To begin Live View, click the Lv button in the center of the Live View option box. To change the white balance settings, turn the rear Main command wheel while holding down the WB button on top of the camera. Press the WB button again to ensure you picked the correct choice.
2. Pressing left on the Multi-selection pad allows you to fine-tune the blue (B) WB number. Similarly, tapping right on the Multi-selection pad allows you to adjust the amber (A) WB number. The range of changeable values is B0.0 to B6.0 or A0.0 to A6.0.
3. Pressing up on the Multi-selection pad changes the green (G) WB number. To change the magenta (M) WB setting, press down on the multi-selection pad. From G0.0 to G6.0 or M0.0 to M6.0, you can modify the value of green or magenta.

How to Fine-Tune White Balance

You can adjust your camera's white balance in increments of 5 mired by adding or subtracting green (G), magenta (M), amber (A), or blue (B) values. Steps of 0.5 and 0.25 mired allow for even minor modifications. Each complete increment (1.0) is around 5 mired; each half-step (0.5) is about 2.5 mired; and each quarter step (0.25) is about 1.25 mired. Each of the four-color changes (A6.0, B6.0, G6.0, and M6.0) allows for up to 30 deep steps. When you've finished fine-tuning, the Control box will display an asterisk (for example, WB*) to indicate that adjustments were made. This star will also appear next to the WB name or sign in the camera's settings and information displays. Note that the star disappears when changes are brought back to zero.

Follow these steps on the Information panel to change the white balance number that Nikon gives you:

1. To get to the Information screen, press the Info button once.

2. To change the White balance setting, hold down the WB button and turn the back Main command dial.

3. The Multi-selection pad lets you fine-tune the amber values (A0.5–A6.0) in 0.5 steps. In the same way, press the right button on the Multi-selection pad to change the blue numbers (B0.5–B6.0) by 0.5 units. To make smaller changes, press up on the Multi-selection pad to change the green values (G0.25–G6.0) and down to change the magenta values (M0.25–M6.0) by 0.25 units each. Watch how the black square moves over the color area as you make changes to get a better idea of how the fine-tuning works.

4. Once the changes are done, let go of the WB button. Now that you've changed the white balance setting on your camera, it will take pictures with that setting until you make more changes. Look at the pictures you took with the new WB value to see how well your tweaking worked.

How to Use the Previous Image's White Balance

You can also choose a white balance choice based on an image you've already taken and use it on pictures you take after that.

To get the white balance setting from a picture on your camera's memory card, do these things:

1. **Access Preset Manual Settings**:
   - o **Action**: Go to the third screen in the menu sequence, select **White Balance**, and then choose **Preset Manual**.
2. **Choose Memory Location**:

- o **Action**: Press the **Multi-selector Center** button to select a memory location for storing the white balance setting from a previously taken picture. This will open the Preset Manual menu. **Note**: Do not press the **OK** button at this stage; pressing OK will only allow you to select the d-1 Preset and will not let you choose a photo already taken.

3. **Navigate to the Preset Manual Menu**:
   - o **Action**: Select an option from the "Preset Manual" menu and move to the right. **Note**: If your memory card is empty, this option will be hidden.

4. **Select the Desired Picture**:
   - o **Action**: The **Select Picture** screen will appear. Browse through your photos to find the one you wish to use for white balance. If necessary, use the **Playback Zoom-In** button to enlarge the image for better viewing. Press the **OK** button to select the picture.

5. **Save and Apply the White Balance Setting**:
   - o **Action**: The chosen picture's white balance setting will be saved to the selected memory spot. The camera will now use this white balance setting until you decide to change it.

Note: This method ensures that the white balance for your current shooting session reflects the lighting conditions of the selected photo, maintaining consistency in your images.

Using the Camera Automatic White Balance Function

The camera includes an automatic white balancing feature that works wonderfully. The camera utilizes an RGB meter to identify the colors in the image and attempts to balance any areas that are white or medium gray. There may be some color discrepancies between images. When you only shoot in Auto WB mode, the camera treats each photograph as if it had a unique white balance issue and performs the appropriate changes without considering previous photos. AUTO0 adjusts the white balance to cold colors, AUTO1 to normal colors, and AUTO2 to brighter colors. Nikon has also included a new mode called Natural Light Auto, which is intended for photographers who want to capture natural scenes. For the majority of shooting situations, AUTO1 is preferable, while AUTO0 and AUTO2 are better for cooler or warmer weather.

To choose an Auto White Balance setting, do the following:

1. In the Shooting menu, select White Balance and then go to the right.

2. To snap images of nature, select Auto or Natural Light Auto from the menu and continue to the right.

3. Move to the right and select one of the three Auto white balance options based on the color warmth you prefer.

Also, select AUTO0 to reduce warm hues in photographs with cooler tones. You can select AUTO2 to maintain the warm tones of the lights or AUTO1 to achieve the standard color rendition. To confirm that you want to keep the white balance setting, press the OK button.

CHAPTER TEN
THE NIKON HISTOGRAM

Along with the exposure meter, the histogram is a useful tool, and in some cases, it may be even more crucial. The exposure meter prepares the camera to take the photograph, and the histogram determines whether the exposure is correct. Even if the exposure meter reading is unavailable or malfunctioning, shooters can still achieve the greatest results by relying solely on the information contained in the histogram. So, the exposure meter and the histogram work together to ensure that every image is correctly lighted and recorded.

Why is it Important to Know How to Use the Histogram?

When you understand the histogram, you will have complete control over where the various light levels appear in their images. This method is akin to the well-known Ansel Adams black-and-white Zone System, but it is displayed visibly on the monitor of high-end cameras like the NIKON Z8. Fine-tuning histogram levels on a computer during post-processing is a vital aspect of working in a digital lab that necessitates careful attention. Being able to edit RAW images on a computer can produce consistently good results, which can help you improve your overall photography skills. The histogram is a quick visual aid that depicts how the image fits into the camera's frame. If the histogram swings too far to the left, the image seems dark and underexposed. If it goes too much to the right, the image seems bright and overexposed. Clipped areas on both ends of the histogram indicate that the image may have been overexposed due to too much light. Mastering the histogram will enhance the quality of your photographs. It's vital to note that the camera's light meter should be utilized for the first exposure alone. After that, photographers can check the histogram to ensure that the image's brightness range falls within the camera's dynamic range. If the histogram exhibits clipped sections on the right or left side, change the exposure or switch to Manual mode to help equal out the light distribution. Take a reading using the light meter to begin, and then utilize the histogram to fine-tune your brightness changes. This procedure ensures that the lighting is just ideal, which increases the overall quality of the final photo.

About the Playback RGB Histogram

The RGB histogram screen, which includes a separate histogram for each color channel, displays in great detail how light is distributed throughout the various color channels. The luminance histogram, which depicts the overall brightness levels in the image, is visible at the top of the RGB histogram. The red, green, and blue (RGB) channels are displayed separately beneath the brightness histogram. This displays how the various color components are distributed in the image. To access the RGB histogram panel, navigate to the Playback Menu on your camera and select Playback display options. After that, select the RGB histogram and check the option to ensure it works. This allows you to turn the RGB bar screen on and off as desired. To view the RGB histogram after turning it on, simply place a photo on the monitor and navigate up or down with the Multi-selection pad. It is critical to examine the RGB histogram to determine whether any color channels have lost information in the image's shadows or highlights. Loss of clarity in certain areas might result in areas that are underexposed or overexposed, lowering the overall image quality. The following section will discuss how to discover spots in a photograph where details may have been lost.

About the Playback Button Luminance Histogram

The RGB histogram screen, which includes a separate histogram for each color channel, displays in great detail how light is distributed throughout the various color channels. The luminance histogram, which depicts the overall brightness levels in the image, is visible at the top of the RGB histogram. The red, green, and blue (RGB) channels are displayed separately beneath the brightness histogram. This displays how the various color components are distributed in the image. To access the RGB histogram panel, navigate to the Playback Menu on your camera and select Playback display options. After that, select the RGB histogram and check the option to ensure it works. This allows you to turn the RGB bar screen on and off as desired. To view the RGB histogram after turning it on, simply place a photo on the monitor and navigate up or down with the Multi-selection pad. It is critical to examine the RGB histogram to determine whether any color channels have lost information in the image's shadows or highlights. Loss of clarity in certain areas might result in areas that are underexposed or overexposed, lowering the overall image quality. The following section will discuss how to discover spots in a photograph where details may have been lost.

About the Highlight (Blink) Mode

In addition to the histogram, the camera offers multiple monitor-watching modes, including the Highlights (blink) mode, which is designed to detect overly bright highlights. To use this feature, navigate to the Playback Menu, select Playback Show

Settings, and then Highlights. When this function is enabled, sections of your image that are too bright to see will flash from light to dark. The blinking effect, which goes from white to black, allows you to observe a histogram with clipped highlight values. This option is useful when shooting quickly and should be used to make quick adjustments to the brightness. Remember that utilizing the light meter, histogram, and Highlights (blink) mode together can give you a lot more control over exposure, allowing you to create photographs with well-exposed highlights that are not clipped.

About the Class-Leading Dynamic Range

"DxO Labs" claims that the camera's image sensor is extremely powerful and can catch a wide range of light values. It boasts an impressive dynamic range of 14.8 EV steps. This makes the NIKON Z8 one of the top cameras in terms of dynamic range, outperforming the Nikon D5's 12.3 EV steps. Before we go any further, take a look at the picture below. A gray area in the center of the image depicts an in-camera histogram. The histogram depicts 256 steps, which reflect the entire range of light levels that your camera can detect. For example, 0 is "pure black" and 255 is "pure white." Colors near the middle of the spectrum are neutral, such as grays, light browns, and greens. Values near the edges are not particularly detailed. The height of the histogram, which commonly resembles a mountain peak or a series of peaks, indicates how much of a specific color is present in the image. It could have a smooth contour, a rounded top, or several peaks. The left side of the histogram displays the darkest values captured by the camera, while the right side displays the brightest values. At the extreme extremes (0 or 255), where the numerals are black or white, characteristics are gone. It's difficult to adjust the peak of the histogram in the camera, but it might help you understand how the colors are distributed. We are mostly interested in the left and right sides of the histogram since we have more control over the dark and light numbers there.

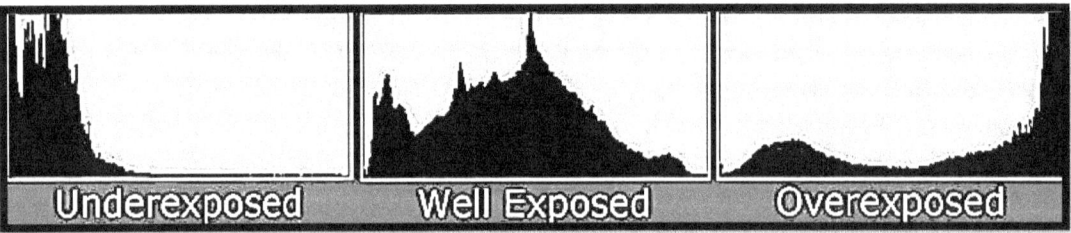

To put it simply, the horizontal scale of the histogram reveals how bright the image is, while the vertical scale shows the colors present. To take well-exposed images, you must understand what the dark and light lines on the horizontal scale imply. If the image appears excessively dark, light values on the histogram's left side will be clipped. Values on the right side will be trimmed if the image appears too light. If the image isn't bright enough, the histogram will be far to the left, stopping at the center peak. In the opposite direction, if the image is correctly lighted, the two edges of the histogram will align with the horizontal sides of the histogram window. If there is too much light, the histogram will shift to the right and be chopped.

CHAPTER ELEVEN

FOCUS/AUTOFOCUS

Understanding the autofocus (AF) choices is critical for fine-tuning the camera's focusing behavior to suit various shooting scenarios, whether you're photographing still or moving subjects. The Automatic Focus Single-Servo (AF-S) setting enables the camera to easily focus on subjects that are stationary or moving slowly. Meanwhile, the Continuous Servo Autofocus (AF-C) mode allows the camera to easily track and keep focus on targets that are constantly moving.

To choose the autofocus mode you want using the viewfinder, just follow these steps:

1. Simply locate and press the AF-mode button on your camera.

2. Adjust the Main command dial situated on the back of the camera.

3. When you rotate the rear dial, the control panel or viewfinder will show you the autofocus configurations available, such as AF-S or AF-C.

4. After the desired mode appears on the Control Panel or viewfinder, press the AF-mode button to confirm your selection.

On the other side, you can select the focusing mode by using the Information display. To reach the Information display, simply hit the info icon on the camera's interface and perform steps 1-3 as described earlier. This alternate way allows users to choose the autofocus setting, giving simplicity and ease of use, especially in fast-paced shooting scenarios where quick adjustments are needed.

The Camera Single-Servo AF Mode (AF-S)

If you're an experienced camera user, you'll know that the single-servo AF (AF-S) mode is ideal for circumstances in which your subject is stationary, such as photographing magnificent landscapes or impressive architectural structures. However, if you're more skilled with cameras, you might choose to use AF-S when photographing subjects that move slowly. Just be cautious of keeping a consistent autofocus performance while the subject is in motion.

Let's see the two scenarios described below to help with decision-making when using this mode:

Subject Remains Static: When you half-push the Shutter-release button or fully press the AF-ON button, the AF module will focus on the stationary subject and wait for your signal to capture the photograph. To verify that the subject is correctly focused before snapping the image, push the Shutter-release button or the AF-ON button with enough pressure. To take the perfect photo, ensure that the subject is perfectly placed within the camera's focus region. This setting is ideal for capturing subjects that are stationary or have very sluggish movement.

Continuous Movement of the Subject: When the subject is constantly moving, even the slightest movement can cause a loss of focus in AF-S mode. For the best focus, consider releasing your finger from the shutter-release button and then half-pressing it again. Alternatively, you can refocus by fully pressing the AF-ON button. It is critical to constantly check and change the focus by repeatedly releasing and half-pushing the shutter-release button or fully pressing the AF-ON button as the subject moves. In most circumstances, it is not recommended to employ AF-S on subjects with continual movement, unpredictable movements, or frequent pauses. For scenarios like these, employing AF-C mode is a preferable alternative because it can track the subject's movement and keep focus locked in continually.

Using the Continuous-Servo AF Mode (AF-C)

Using the camera autofocus (AF) functions for precise focus monitoring can be quite challenging, especially when dealing with subjects moving in different directions.

Below we will analyze three different scenarios to demonstrate these responses:

Static Subject: When the subject is not moving, continuous-servo AF performs similarly to single-servo AF. However, if the focus is not locked, the autofocus motor may make minor changes to the focus point as the camera moves. It is vital to avoid mistakenly changing the active AF point away from the subject, as this can result in the camera focusing on items in the background instead.

Continuous Movement of Subject within the Frame: When the subject moves within the frame, maintaining focus is critical for capturing the right photo. When utilizing Single-point AF area mode, keep your focus on the subject no matter how it moves. If you select Dynamic-area AF or Auto-area AF, the camera will be able to easily track the subject, either inside a specific group of focus points or throughout the complete range of possible focus points. In the following part, we will go over AF-Area Modes in detail.

The Subject Approaches or Recedes: When the subject approaches or moves away from the camera, the cameras predictive focus tracking function activates automatically. Predictive Focus Tracking is a feature that allows you to anticipate the movement of the subject's distance before pressing the shutter button. Before snapping the shot, the camera's predictive focus tracking technology makes minor modifications to the lens elements to ensure that they are exactly aligned with the subject's projected position. When the subject comes into view, the lens changes its focus slightly in advance to ensure precise focus when the image sensor takes the shot.

Setting and Using the AF Area Modes

The AF-area setups are critical for controlling your camera's focus. Adjusting the active number of Viewfinder AF points allows you to specify the area of focus and prioritize what the camera focuses on. This function is extremely useful while working with moving subjects because it makes it easier to monitor and focus on them. Three of the four modes available are designed expressly to track the subject's movement. Single-point AF mode allows you to focus with precision on a single AF point. If you desire a larger focus area, the Group-area AF option expands it to nine AF points. Dynamic-area AF mode increases flexibility by providing several alternatives for AF locations, allowing for improved response to varying amounts of subject movement. The 3D-tracking mode is particularly effective for recording dynamic subjects. With an amazing 153 AF points, it employs color information to track and focus on moving subjects with extreme precision. The Auto AF-area mode automatically selects the ideal AF-area mode for you, removing the need for manual adjustments.

Below is a step-by-step guide to selecting an AF-area mode:
1. Fully press the AF-mode button.
2. Use the front sub-command dial to easily cycle through the various AF-area modes indicated on the control panel.
3. Once your preferred mode shows on the Control Panel, just press the AF-mode button again to confirm your choice.

When you set your camera to Single-servo AF mode (AF-S), you can only use Single-point AF, Group-area AF, and Auto-area AF as AF-area modes. Similarly, if you select Continuous-servo AF mode (AF-C), you will be unable to use certain AF-area modes, including 3D-Tracking, 25-point Dynamic-area AF, 72-point Dynamic-area AF, and 153-point Dynamic-area AF. To access the majority of AF-area choices, ensure that your camera is set to AF-C. If you wish to fine-tune both the Autofocus mode and the AF-area mode at the same time, simply hold down the AF-mode button and use the rear

Main command dial for Autofocus, while the front Sub-command dial handles the AF-area mode. Now, let's explore each AF-area mode to obtain a thorough grasp of their unique features.

How to Use the Single Point AF to Get Proper Focus

Single-Point AF is a mode that allows you to precisely choose one of 153 available AF points. As previously indicated, you can alter the active AF point with either the Sub-selector joystick or the Multi-selector pad. Consider a circumstance in which two subjects are positioned adjacent to one other, with a short gap between them. In such cases, a single center AF point can be used to determine the distance between them.

Here's a helpful approach to focusing in such situations:

Option 1: To capture the perfect shot, make sure to focus on the subjects' faces by aiming the center AF point at them. Press and hold the shutter-release button halfway to initiate the focusing process, and then you can recompose the shot as desired. Keep the shutter button halfway pressed to ensure the focus is locked, adjust your frame as needed, and then fully press the button to capture the perfect shot.

Option 2: Alternatively, you might start by fine-tuning the composition such that the subject is in the middle of the frame. Then, using the Multi-selector pad or Sub-selector joystick, precisely set the single AF point so that it is exactly aligned with the subject's face. After moving the AF point, partially push the shutter release button to establish fine focus before fully pressing it to snap the photo. When utilizing Single-Point AF mode, keep the following things in mind: When utilizing Single-Point AF, the Viewfinder will only show one AF point. With the Multi-select pad, you can relocate this point to any of the 55 AF point locations. These places are represented with larger AF point squares rather than the smaller dots found within them. With this function, you have complete control over where the focal point is positioned in the frame, providing you with greater versatility when creating your images.

The Group-area AF

Group-area AF improves autofocus reliability by combining many AF sites rather than relying on only one. Contrary to what was previously said, Group-area AF employs a cross-pattern of nine AF points, however only four are often shown in the Viewfinder. Understanding the importance of a cross-pattern of AF points is essential while discussing this subject. This technique is quite useful in circumstances when the camera may become distracted by the background or other elements surrounding the subject. In some cases, the AF points are deliberately positioned to catch a portion of the subject without requiring additional changes. This makes the cross-pattern ideal for shooting subjects that are difficult to focus on with a single AF point. Furthermore, when you enable Face detection in the Custom Setting Menu > b Metering/Exposure > b5 Matrix metering and utilize AF-S Autofocus mode with Matrix metering, the camera becomes expert at recognizing human faces through the Viewfinder.

This tool is particularly handy for recording unique moments during weddings, graduations, and portrait sessions. When you look through the viewfinder, you'll discover a cross-pattern comprised of four visible autofocus (AF) points and five hidden AF points. You can move the cluster of nine AF points around within the array of 153 AF points displayed in the Viewfinder. This is easily accomplished using either the Multi-selector pad or the Sub-selector. These nine parameters, together with a thorough grasp of the subject's attributes and the use of matrix metering mode, significantly improve subject identification accuracy. Group-area AF, on the other hand, limits the number of cross-pattern AF points shown in the viewfinder to four.

However, you may quickly move this pattern across the Viewfinder using the Multi-selector pad or Sub-selector, which are conveniently situated among the 55 AF point selections. With this level of versatility, you'll have complete control over the focus region, resulting in improved focusing accuracy regardless of the shooting conditions.

The Dynamic-Area AF

Dynamic-area AF mode is very good at capturing subjects in continuous motion. This mode allows you to make use of a flexible range of AF points structured in a selected pattern, improving focusing efficiency to keep up with fast-moving subjects. It's important to remember that using this option requires the AF-C Autofocus mode (Continuous-servo AF). When the camera is in AF-S Autofocus mode (single-servo AF), the Control Panel will not display the Dynamic-area AF mode choice. The Dynamic-area AF tab in the Control Panel provides various point-setting options, giving you more focusing versatility. The configurations are displayed in the top row of the image. To select one of the four AF-point patterns, twist the front Sub-command dial while holding the AF-mode trigger. When you look through the viewfinder, you will notice a row at the bottom that shows the pattern of four autofocus points you've chosen (9, 25, 72, or 153). When shooting, keep in mind that not all additional AF spots will light up. They will only appear when a pattern is first picked. Understanding the significance of perceiving nearby points that may not be visible in the Viewfinder is critical since they play an important part in improving autofocus effectiveness. Furthermore, using the Multi-selector pad or Sub-selector, you may simply manipulate the 9-point, 25-point, and 72-point patterns in the Viewfinder.

To guarantee that the subject moves as little as possible, the 153-point pattern uses all available autofocus points. Keep in mind that, while the main autofocus is decided by the AF point displayed in the Viewfinder, the surrounding points in the selected pattern remain active. If the subject changes or the primary autofocus point loses focus, another point in the area immediately takes over. Choosing a smaller number of AF points, such as 9 or 25, is great for catching subjects that move slowly or often. However, if the subject's motion becomes more irregular or unpredictable, consider increasing the number of AF points to 72 or 153. This will enhance the camera's tracking performance, particularly in unexpected or urgent situations. When shooting in low light, selecting a higher number of AF points may result in a slightly slower initial autofocus reaction. Once focus is established, the camera is excellent at tracking the object utilizing all three patterns. In a word, dynamic-area AF enables the accurate tracking and capture of subjects of varying sizes, shapes, and speeds. It's worth noting that having 153 points may slightly slow down the initial focus reaction time since the camera has more details to analyze.

The 3D-Tracking AF

The 3D-tracking AF mode, which is prominently stated in the Control Panel, Information Display, and Viewfinder, improves accuracy by including color detection in the tracking system. This mode excels in precisely tracking the subject area and uses the subject's color hue to boost its tracking capabilities. The 153-point Dynamic-area AF pattern particularly shines when it comes to demonstrating the intelligence of the 3D-tracking mode. This camera's innovative color-based technology ensures remarkable accuracy, particularly in adverse lighting conditions where the subject's color shows out against the background. It's worth noting that when the subject and background are the same color, automated focus tracking may not operate as well. It's worth noting that activities like sporting events, air displays, and racing are ideal for taking advantage of the 3D-tracking feature. This setting improves the camera's capabilities by allowing it to track subjects and capture their colors precisely. When 3D tracking is enabled, the Viewfinder displays "3 D" while holding down the AF-mode button. With its sophisticated tracking capabilities, the camera effortlessly selects the best AF point from a list of 153 alternatives. In the Viewfinder, you'll see a dot-centered square or object that serves as a visual indicator for tracking the subject's movements. This square or dot reacts to any motion initiated by the subject within the Viewfinder and provides real-time feedback on tracking performance.

The Auto-Area AF

This setting allows you to easily snap breathtaking photographs without the need for manual focusing. The AF option takes charge, intelligently selecting the most appropriate AF point or points for your subject. This mode, which has lenses labeled D, E, or G, employs advanced "person recognition technology." Your camera's Auto-area AF feature detects human faces with remarkable accuracy, even in cluttered backgrounds. Furthermore, when a face is recognized, the camera's settings will automatically adapt to provide the greatest available lighting, which is very handy when photographing in low light or difficult lighting conditions. Using Auto-area AF mode and clicking the AF-mode button can make the procedure even faster. The Viewfinder provides a more streamlined perspective of the 153 AF points by removing the AF point's primary display. It's fascinating how the choice of AF-S or AF-C Autofocus mode affects how AF points show during autofocus. When utilizing AF-S Autofocus mode, the camera shows a random arrangement of AF points that are focused on the subject. It carefully analyzes the scene, determines the best focus point, and seamlessly tracks the subject, ensuring perfect sharpness and clarity in every photograph. In contrast, when utilizing AF-C Autofocus mode, the camera expertly follows the subject's movement by continually adjusting focus, with a single AF point dynamically moving across the Viewfinder. When you hold the shutter release button halfway down in AF-C mode, the AF point continues to test focus without locking onto a single point. This dynamic adjustment delivers a continually sharp and impeccably focused photo, even when the subject moves within the frame.

CHAPTER TWELVE

GENERAL TIPS AND PRINCIPLES TO KEEP IN MIND WHEN SHOOTING IN VARIOUS SCENARIOS

When Shooting Portrait

Here are some principles and practical tips for capturing breathtaking portraits:

Depth of Field

- Understanding how to achieve a shallow depth of field is essential for creating engaging pictures. Select the smallest aperture available for your lens, such as f/2.8 or f/4.

- Use aperture priority mode to have control over the aperture setting while the camera takes care of other exposure parameters.

Pay close attention to the eyes

- Make sure the eyes are in sharp focus since they are the focal point of portrait photography.
- Utilize single-point autofocus or manual focus for precise focusing on the subject's eyes, which will enhance the overall impact of the image.

Adjusting Exposure Compensation

- To fine-tune an image's brightness, utilize exposure compensation.
- Adjust the exposure compensation to either brighten or darken the image, allowing for the best possible exposure for your portrait.

Managing Shutter Speed and ISO

- To prevent graininess caused by slow shutter speeds, you can increase the ISO to enhance the sensor's sensitivity to light.
- - Understanding ISO settings helps capture clear shots with little motion blur. Increasing the ISO allows you to attain higher shutter speeds, which results in crisper photographs.

Selecting the Perfect Focal Length

- Choosing a focal length of 50mm or longer can help reduce distortion and bring out the best features of your subject.
- Longer focal lengths create a pleasing perspective compression, which leads to portraits that look more natural and have less distortion.

When Shooting a Group Portrait

Here are some principles and expert advice for capturing amazing group portraits:

Depth of Field

- Maintaining group concentration requires a deep depth of field. For the best results, put your aperture between f/8 and f/16.
- Use aperture priority mode to have control over the aperture setting while letting the camera handle other exposure parameters.

Focusing

- Pay close attention to the person in the center of the group, making sure they are sharply in focus.
- To ensure correct focus, use the Zoom tool to magnify the image and study faces in both front and rear rows.
- To ensure that all subjects remain sharp and in focus, consider adjusting to a smaller aperture. This will increase the depth of field and help eliminate any blurriness that may occur.

Take into consideration the lighting conditions: Consider the lighting conditions throughout the entire scene when framing your group portrait. Make use of matrix metering for precise exposure throughout the entire frame.

Organizing the Group

- - Arrange the group to ensure visibility through the viewfinder. Furthermore, ensure that they are positioned such that each member has a clear view of the camera.
- Pay attention to the composition and make sure that people are positioned in a balanced and visually appealing way within the frame.

Exposure Adjustment

- Keep a close eye on the exposure levels and make necessary adjustments to compensate for any areas that are too bright or too dark.
- Adjust the exposure settings to ensure well-balanced lighting and preserve all the intricate details in both the bright and dark areas.

Managing Haze: If you're experiencing haziness in your photos, you might want to try increasing the ISO to achieve a faster shutter speed. This feature minimizes motion blur and enhances image sharpness, particularly in outdoor or difficult lighting situations.

Tips for Capturing Stunning Landscape Photos

Here are some tricks and expert tips that will help you capture breathtaking landscape photographs:

Achieving Maximum Depth of Field

- Begin by using a narrow aperture setting of f/16 to achieve a deep depth of field, which will result in sharp focus from the foreground to the background.

- Use aperture priority mode to have control over the aperture setting while allowing the camera to handle other exposure parameters.

Stabilization

- Invest in a reliable tripod to reduce camera shake and obtain clear shots, especially in tricky lighting or long exposure techniques.
- It's important to disable vibration reduction (VR) on both the camera body and lens when using a tripod. This will prevent any image blur that may occur due to VR compensating for movement that doesn't exist.

Metering and Autofocus

- Choose matrix metering mode for precise evaluation of the lighting conditions in the scene and automatic adjustment of exposure settings.
- Utilize the AF-S focus mode for precise focusing on your desired subject, be it a distant mountain range or a nearby rock formation.

Managing Digital Noise Control: To reduce digital noise and maintain image quality, keep the ISO level between 64-200, especially when shooting in well-lit outdoor environments with abundant natural light.

Shooting in RAW Format: Take images in RAW format to preserve the highest level of detail and provide additional editing possibilities later. RAW files contain unprocessed data directly from the camera's sensor, giving you more flexibility in modifying exposure, white balance, and color grading throughout the editing process.

When Shooting Still or Freeze Action Photography

Here are some tips and techniques for capturing dynamic and fast-moving subjects:

Proper Use of Shutter Speed

- To effectively freeze motion, you can adjust the shutter speed by selecting shutter priority mode (S or TV mode).
- To capture clean and clear shots without motion blur, set your shutter speed to 1/500 to 1/8000 seconds, depending on the subject's movement.

Continuous Autofocus (AF-C)

- Utilize AF-C or continuous autofocus mode to ensure the camera maintains focus on a subject that is in motion.
- - Continuous autofocus maintains a sharp focus on moving subjects. It's like having a camera expert by your side, constantly changing the focus to take the ideal photo.

Exposure and ISO

- If you're experiencing an underexposed or grainy image, you might want to consider adjusting the ISO sensitivity.
- Alternatively, you can choose AUTO ISO mode to let the camera adjust the ISO settings automatically according to the lighting conditions. This ensures that you get the best exposure without compromising the quality of your images.

Tips for Capturing Blur or Motion Panning Scenarios

Here are some valuable tips and techniques for capturing dynamic and moving subjects:

Experiment with Shutter Speed

- - Use slower shutter speeds to create a sense of movement in your images. Select shutter priority mode (S or TV mode) to control the shutter speed while the camera automatically adjusts other exposure settings.
- Experiment with slowing down the shutter speed to capture a hint of motion in your photos, giving them a vibrant and energetic touch.

Tracking Subject Movement: Before capturing the photo, you should anticipate your subject's movement and track it within the frame. By following these procedures, you may ensure that the subject remains in the appropriate position and maintains focus during the exposure.

Using Live View: You might wish to try your camera's live view feature. It allows you to track the subject's movement in real-time while capturing the photo. This tool allows you to create more accurate framing and composition, especially when shooting subjects in motion.

Autofocus: Use the dynamic-area AF and continuous autofocus (AF-C) technologies to easily keep your subject in focus even when it's moving. Dynamic-area AF allows you to select a specific region to focus on, whereas AF-C ensures that the focus is constantly altered to keep up with the subject's movement.

When Shooting in Low-Light Scenarios

Here are some helpful tips and techniques:

Selecting the Perfect Aperture: Opt for a wide aperture, like f/2.8 or f/4, to capture a shallow depth of field and create a stunningly blurred background. Optimize your camera settings by selecting aperture priority mode (A or Av). This mode grants you control over the aperture while enabling the camera to automatically adjust other exposure settings.

Learning how to use Exposure with Spot Metering: When photographing a subject's face, particularly in difficult lighting conditions, consider using spot metering mode. This provides accurate exposure by metering the light, particularly on the subject's face, preventing any potential difficulties with over or underexposure.

Autofocus: Use a single autofocus (AF) point along with continuous autofocus (AF-C) mode to ensure that your subject remains in sharp focus, particularly when capturing portraits with movement or in dynamic surroundings.

ISO Sensitivity

- To optimize exposure and reduce digital noise in low-light circumstances, set the ISO sensitivity to 1600 or higher, taking into account available light.
- Raising the ISO setting enables a quicker shutter speed, resulting in the ability to freeze action and capture more detailed photos, especially in low-light conditions.

When Shooting a Long Exposure Scenario

Here are some useful guidelines to improve your long-exposure photography:

Mastering Long Exposures: For exposures longer than 30 seconds, switch to manual photography mode and use the bulb shutter speed. This feature gives you entire control over the exposure period, which is ideal for capturing amazing effects like light trails or star trails.

Achieving Stability with a Tripod: For the best results and to reduce any unwanted movement, it is recommended to utilize a reliable tripod for optimal stability. Make sure to turn off the vibration reduction function on both the camera and lens to avoid any unintentional blurring in your long exposure shots.

Autofocus: If you're familiar with cameras, you might wish to attempt manual focus or the single autofocus (AF-S) mode when shooting in low light. This ensures accurate focus, especially when taking static subjects over extended exposures.

Capturing High-Quality RAW Images

- Shooting in RAW format will help you preserve the maximum amount of detail and give you more flexibility for post-processing. This file format preserves all the image data captured by the camera sensor, giving you more flexibility to adjust exposure, color, and other parameters during the editing process.
- It is advisable to maintain a low ISO setting (between 64 and 400) to reduce digital noise and capture images of superior quality, characterized by exceptional clarity and sharpness.

Reducing Camera Shake: To minimize camera shake during long exposures, it's best to refrain from directly touching the camera. Instead, utilize a cable release with a lock function to remotely activate the shutter, guaranteeing optimal stability and sharpness in your images.

CHAPTER THIRTEEN

NIKON MOVIE RECORDING/MOVIE SHOOTING MENU

Basic Operations of Movie Recording and Playback

Getting ready to record

- Press the camera screen to start recording a movie.
- Keep an eye on the screen to see how much movie recording time is left.
- The movie frame (2), which shows the area to be recorded in the movie, should be shown.

Initiating Recording

- To begin recording a movie, press the movie-record button.
- When the camera is on, it starts to record and focuses in the middle of the frame.
- Tap the Pause/Play button to stop recording and press it again to start again. Keep in mind that the recording stops after about five minutes of pause unless you choose the HS movie choice.

Ending the Recording: If you want to stop recording, tap the "end" button.

Playback: To pick and play movies, go to full-frame viewing mode. Use the movie choices icon to find movies.

Focusing during recording

- Modify the focus while recording a movie based on the Autofocus mode setting in the movie menu:
- **"Single AF":** means that the focus locks when the recording starts. During recording, use the multi-selector to start focusing.
- "Full-time AF": The camera's focus is constantly changed while it's recording. If you set the AE/AF lock button, the focus lock button will be different. Press the button to lock the view while you're recording, and then press it again to open it.

Manually Adjust the Focus: Rotate the side dial to change the focus by hand while recording a movie when the focus mode switch is set to manual focus.

Control of Exposure

- The exposure lock setting in the setup screen determines how the movie is locked during recording:
- Tap the AE/AF lock button to lock exposure while recording if AE/AF lock, AE lock only, or AE lock (Hold) is chosen. To open, press the button.
- The multi-selector can be used to lock brightness while recording for [AF lock only]. To open, press the AE/AF lock button again.

Maximum Movie Recording Time

- The shot screen shows how much time is left to record a single movie, which is useful information for people who are filming.
- Each movie file can't be longer than 29 minutes, no matter how much space is on the memory card. Each file can only be 4 GB, even if there's plenty of space for longer records. If a file is bigger than 4 GB, it is automatically split into several smaller files so that it can't be played continuously.
- If the camera's temperature rises a lot while it's working, the recording time may be shorter than the maximum time.
- The real amount of time left to record may be different depending on the movie, how the subject moves, or the type of memory card that was used.
- - For optimal video recording results, use memory cards with an SD Speed Class rate of 6 (Video Speed Class V6) or faster. If you want to record in [2160/30p] or [2160/25p] (4K UHD) codecs, use memory cards with a UHS Speed Class of 3 (Video Speed Class V30) or above. Using lower-rated cards could cause the recording to be interrupted unexpectedly.

Notes on Camera Temperature

- The camera may get hot if you use it in hot places or for long periods while making movies.
- - The camera will automatically stop recording if it reaches a certain temperature during filming. There is a timer that indicates how many seconds remain till the recording stops. The camera turns off after the recording is over.
- If the camera gets too hot, it should be turned off until it is cool enough to use.

Notes on Recording Movies

Saving Pictures or Videos: While saving, LEDs indicating the number of frames or minutes remaining may flash, and a notice stating "Please wait for the camera to finish recording." may appear. If you do not want to lose data or harm the camera or memory card, don't open the battery chamber/memory card slot cover or remove the battery or memory card while these lights are on.

Recorded Movies

- When recording a movie, you can capture various working sounds, including zoom control, side dial, autofocus lens movement, shaking reduction, and aperture modifications due to light changes.
- The following things can happen when you save movies/videos:
- Images taken with fluorescent, mercury-vapor, or sodium-vapor lights might have bands on them.
- Things that move quickly, like trains or cars passing the frame, may be skewed.
- If you pan the camera, the whole movie picture might look off.
- Images from bright places may stay on the screen even when the camera is moving.
- When recording or playing back a movie, colorful lines may appear on repeating patterns, such as textiles or lattice windows, depending on the subject's distance and zoom level. This occurs because the subject's pattern and the structure of the image sensor do not work well together. It is not indicative of a problem.

Autofocus to Record Movies: Autofocus may not work as well as expected in some situations with objects that aren't good for autofocus. To deal with this:
- Before you start making a movie, go to the movie menu and find the Autofocus mode. Choose Single AF (the usual setting) or a different mode.
- - To improve focus, place another topic in the middle of the frame that is around the same distance from the camera as the main subject. Begin recording and make adjustments to the arrangement as necessary.

Types of Video Files

To choose the type of video file, go to the menu for capturing videos and choose [Video file type].

There are three versions to choose from: NEV, MOV, and MP4. Below are list of options:

N-RAW 12-bit (NEV): This format is intended for footage to be processed and edited in RAW on high-end machines used in professional video editing. A "proxy video" is an H.264 8-bit MP4 video recorded at a frame size of 1920 × 1080 for playback on the camera. It includes two-tone modes: [SDR] and [N-Log], and the "Video quality (N-

RAW)" option allows you to adjust the quality. The sound is recorded using linear pulse code modulation (PCM).

ProRes RAW HQ 12-bit (MOV): This format is designed for professional video editors to process and edit RAW files on high-performance computers. It can record H.264 8-bit MP4 videos at 1920 × 1080 resolution for camera viewing. It has two tone modes, [SDR] and [N-Log], and records sound in PCM format.

ProRes 422 HQ 10-bit (MOV): This file has two tone modes, [SDR] and [N-Log], and is best for footage that will be edited after the fact. All-I intra-frame compression is used during the recording process, and music is saved in PCM format.

H265 10-bit (MOV): This format features three tone modes—[SDR], [HLG], and [N-Log]—and is designed to be used with video clips created on high-performance computers in professional video editing. Video is recorded using Long GOP inter-frame compression, while music is recorded in PCM format.

H.265 8-bit (MOV): This format is known for being very good at compression. It saves video using long GOP inter-frame compression and music in PCM format. You can only choose SDR as the tone mode.

H.264 8-bit (MP4): This is a file type that is widely accepted. It records using long GOP inter-frame compression, and the audio is saved in AAC format.

Choose a Tone Mode

To choose the tone mode, pick [N-RAW 12-bit (NEV)], [ProRes RAW HQ 12-bit (MOV)], [ProRes 422 HQ 10-bit (MOV)], or [H.265 10-bit (MOV)] and hit "Ok." Make sure that the option you select matches your needs. Remember that movies created in H.265 8-bit (MOV) and H.264 8-bit (MP4) codecs can only be played in SDR, so you can't choose a tone mode.

Below is the list of options:
- **SDR**: The standard Dynamic Range setting allows you to select from a typical range of light levels, commonly known as the dynamic range.
- **HLG**: The camera supports high dynamic range (HDR) and has a greater range of dynamic contrast than SDR. Only supports [H.265 10-bit (MOV)].
- **N-Log**: This mode uses a unique logarithmic curve to capture images with a large dynamic range. When applied after production, 3D LUTs for N-Log curves can provide attractive pictures that operate on a reference monitor.

Color Space

In the video recording settings, you can choose from the following video color spaces, frame widths, frame rates, bit rates, and quality options: The following video color

spaces are linked to **the Video file type settings for [H.265 10-bit (MOV)], [H.265 8-bit (MOV)], and [H.264 8-bit (MP4)]:**
- BT.709 (SDR)
- BT.2100 [HLG]
- BT.2020 [N-Log]

Frame Size and Rate Options

From the menu for recording videos, users can choose the frame rate and frame size they want. **What frame sizes are possible depends on the settings for the [Video file type]. Also, see the options below:**
- The [FX] image area records "FX" options no matter what setting you choose for [Image area] > [Choose image area]. The [DX] image area records "DX" options as well. If you choose the "2.3x" option, the apparent focal length is about 2.3 times longer than with the FX version.
- When a DX lens is attached, the DX-based video file is automatically chosen, so "FX" choices can't be chosen.

Furthermore, there are different frame rates for 120p, 100p, 60p, 50p, 30p, 25p, and 24p, with speeds of 119.88 fps for 120p, 100 fps for 100p, 59.94 fps for 50p, 29.97 fps for 25p, and 23.976 fps for 24p. In the video recording choices, [Electronic VR] must be set to [OFF]. Videos are saved in 8K Ultra High Definition (UHD) format except when DX lenses are utilized, in which case they are saved in 4K UHD.

Bit Rate

The bit rate changes based on the kind of video file:
- If you choose **Video quality (N-RAW)** in the video recording screen, the bit rate of [N-RAW 12-bit (NEV)] will depend on that.
- **N-RAW 12-Bit NEV with High Quality and Normal Quality**: There are mean bit rates given for both NEV and MP4 movies when the "High quality" and "Normal quality" options for "Video quality (N-RAW)" are selected.
- **Quality of the video (N-RAW):** Through the video recording screen, users can pick the video file type [N RAW 12-bit (NEV)] and the quality level [High quality] or [Normal].

ISO Sensitivity Settings

Change the ISO sensitivity settings so that they work well with video mode. Here are the options available:

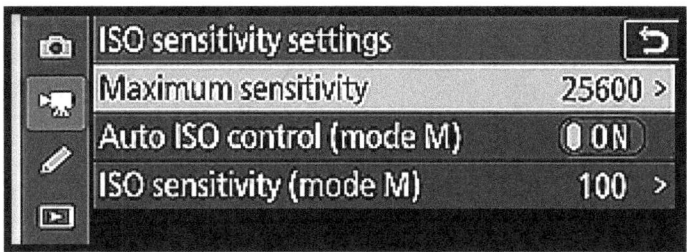

Maximum sensitivity

- Choose the highest resolution to make the camera work better. You can pick from ISO 200 to Hi 2.0.
- This chosen number sets the highest ISO sensitivity that can be used in P, S, and A modes, as well as when [Auto ISO control (mode M)] is turned on in mode M.

Auto control ISO (mode M)

- **ON:** If you choose this option, auto ISO control will be turned on in mode M.
- **OFF:** Keep the ISO sensitivity number you set by hand for mode M.
- The auto ISO sensitivity control works in modes other than M, no matter what setting is chosen.

ISO Sensitivity (mode M): Pick the ISO setting between ISO 64 and Hi 2.0 while the camera is in mode M.

Notes on the Auto ISO Sensitivity Control

- "Noise" may get worse at high ISO settings, showing up as bright pixels, haze, or lines that are spread out randomly.
- High ISO settings might make it harder for the camera to focus. It's best to choose a smaller number for the [Maximum sensitivity] setting in the [ISO sensitivity settings] to avoid these problems.

HLG Quality

To get the finest HLG (Hybrid Log-Gamma) image processing, select HLG as the tone mode in the Video file type > H.265 10-bit (MOV) options in the video recording menu.

Here are the options available:

Quick Sharp: The Quick Sharp tool lets you make quick edits to get a good improvement in Sharpening, Mid-range sharpening, and Clarity.

Sharpening: Modify the amount of sharpness so that both the image's edges and its finer features are just right.

Mid-range sharpening: Use the sharpening and clarity tools to change how sharp patterns and lines are.

Clarity: Make the picture clearer by changing how sharp the general image parts are as well as how thick the edges are while keeping the brightness and dynamic range the same.

Contrast: Modify the contrast to get the best mix of dark and light places.

Saturated: Modify the brightness to change how intense the colors are, making them brighter or less bright as needed.

Hue: Fine-tune the hue to change the general tone of the color, which lets you make precise color changes.

Active D-Lighting

To make your movies look better, keep the features in both the bright highlights and the deep blacks. This will create a natural contrast.

Here are the options available:

Extra High, High, Normal, and Low

- Users are given some options for adjusting the level of Active D-Lighting, which lets them make it fit their needs.
- There are four levels of Active D-Lighting, from the highest (Extra high) to the lowest (Low). Pick the level that works best for you.

OFF: Turn off the Active D-Lighting tool to keep the contrast as it is and not make it better.

Video Flicker Reduction

If you want to reduce flicker and bands in both your shooting screen and taped footage, especially when using fluorescent or mercury-vapor lights, follow these steps:

Auto: Make it possible for the camera to instantly find the right frequency to fix flicker and banding problems.

[50 Hz] or [60 Hz]:
- To get the results you want, if the "Auto" choice doesn't work, choose [50 Hz] or [60 Hz] by hand, depending on the frequency of your power supply.
- Pick [50 Hz] for places where the power supply frequency is 50 Hz and [60 Hz] for places where it is 60 Hz. For best efficiency, it's important to match the frequency of the power source.

Notes:

- If you're unsure about the local power supply frequency and the [Auto] option doesn't work, try both 50 and 60 Hz settings. Choose the one that will offer you the greatest results.
- Flicker reduction might not work when the image is too bright. To fix this, you might want to use a smaller lens with a higher f-number.
- - Flicker reduction efficiency may vary depending on the mode. For uniform results, utilize mode M and select a shutter speed that matches the frequency of the power source:
- Time lengths of 1/100 s, 1/50 s, and 1/25 s at 50 Hz.
- At a frequency of 60 Hz, the period is 1/125 s, the cycle lasts 1/60 s, and the half-cycle lasts 1/30s.

Also, do not forget that changes you make to the Video flicker reduction feature affect both the live video and the video you record, even if you are in photo mode.

High-Frequency Flicker Reduction

By enabling the On (shutter speed fine-tuning) setting, users can adjust shutter speeds in mode M from ±s to ±s. This allows you to make precise adjustments, assisting you in determining the ideal shutter speeds for reducing flicker. Users can also see a copy of the photo on the camera display, which helps them determine the appropriate shutter speed.

AF Options for Subject Detection

Subject Detection: You can tell the camera what kind of image to focus on when it's in video mode, which lets you make the autofocus work better in certain situations.

When Subject Not Detected

- Find out what the camera does when it can't find a subject of the type you chose under Subject Detection while the focus mode is set to Full-time AF.
- **ON**: Autofocus stays on even if the subject type you chose isn't found, so the camera can keep tracking the focus.
- **OFF**: Turns off autofocus when the chosen subject type isn't found, giving you control over how the camera focuses in those cases.

Wind Noise Reduction

Press the ON button to activate the low-cut filter and eliminate wind noise from the built-in microphone. It's vital to remember that turning on this filter may also modify other noises. **Also note the following:**
- The audio mics that can be added do not change when the Wind noise reduction option is turned on.
- Users can turn on or off wind noise reduction for audio mics that have it built in by using the microphone adjustments. This gives you the freedom to control wind noise reduction based on your recording needs.

CHAPTER FOURTEEN

QUICK START CHECKLIST FOR VIDEO RECORDING

The following ideas are very important to remember as you work to improve your filmmaking skills and make more videos. **Some of them are outlines of the information you learned about taking still shots, while others are more focused on making movies in video format.**

- **Stills too**. By pressing the shutter release button on your camera, you can shoot a high-resolution, edited still shot while also recording a video. If you accidentally stop recording video, neither still images nor video frames are lost. If you select the JPEG quality option, you can stretch the still image to the same 16:9 ratio as your video and save it at the same resolution as the frame size. HD mode produces photographs with a resolution of 1920 x 1080 (2 megapixels), whilst UHD (4K) mode produces images with a resolution of 3840 x 2160 (8 megapixels). When you push the shutter release button on your camera to start recording a movie in Continuous release mode, only one photo is taken. It's feasible to employ up to fifty distinct takes to make one movie.
- **No flash**. When the image selector switch is in the Movie position, you can still take pictures while recording video, but the flash will not work.
- **Exposure compensation**. The exposure compensation can be modified to increase or decrease exposure by 3 EV for every 1/3 EV. It's vital to understand that the range for still images is plus or minus 5 EV.

- **Size Does Matter**. Regardless of the quality setting, a single video clip can be up to 4 gigabytes in size and no more than 29 minutes and 59 seconds. A movie can consist of up to eight distinct files, each of which is four gigabytes in size. No matter what frame size and frame rate you select, the quantity and length of files created will vary. The size or duration of your files may also be limited by the speed and space available on your memory card.
- **Pick the right card**. Use a fast XQD card if feasible. If you insist on using a slower card, the recording may stop after a few minutes, even though full HD requires a transfer rate of 28 Mbps, HD can take 56 Mbps, and 4K takes 144 Mbps. In any case, select a memory card capable of holding at least 32 gigabytes. Although some older XQD cards can contain up to 16 GB, it is unlikely that High Quality will operate with them.
- **Purchase a wireless external microphone**. If you want the best sound quality and to avoid picking up zoom or tracking motor noise by accident, buy a stereo microphone that is different from your camera.
- **Minimize zooming**. Although it is cool to be able to zoom in on a distant thing and have it fill the entire screen, you should proceed with utmost caution. If you don't utilize an external microphone, you'll hear the zoom ring rotating every time you watch a video. Friends who watch your movies will be upset if you zoom in too much at times. Additionally, using digital zoom will result in lower-quality images. Avoid utilizing digital zoom if keeping good image quality is more essential to you than getting close to a certain subject, such as a famous actor or actress.
- **Be sure the battery is fully charged**. A brand-new battery will last approximately 85 minutes under typical conditions. However, if there are frequent attention changes, this time may be reduced. Because of this, a single film can only be 29 minutes long.
- **Keep it cool**. Heat can damage the image sensor, so store the camera somewhere cold while not in use. On extremely hot days, the camera sensor may warm up more quickly during shooting. If this happens, the camera will stop recording immediately and turn off after around five seconds. Let it cool before using it again.
- **Just click the video button**. You do not need to hold it with your hand. When you're done, you can stop the recording by hitting it one more time.

Shooting Your Movie

Now let us take a closer look at the steps the Nikon Z8 takes to record your video:

- o **Connect the Microphone**: The microphone socket on the left side of the camera can be used with an external monoaural or stereo microphone that has a 3.5mm stereo mini plug.
- o **Pick the Exposure Mode:** You Want To Use: Look at the last step's information to assist you choose an exposure mode, such as Program, shutter priority, aperture priority, or Manual exposure. The Z8 employs matrix metering, a method for calculating exposure that considers sensor data.
- o **Change the exposure**: The changes you can make will depend on the exposure mode you choose. For example,
  - ▪ To modify the exposure in Program/Shutter-priority mode, push the EV button on top of the camera and crank the main command dial. This can be accomplished by switching to program/shutter priority mode. The Z8 fully controls the ISO sensitivity level and shutter speed.
  - ▪ Concentrate on the aperture. You can adjust the f-stop by using the sub-command dial. To alter the exposure, push the EV button and then turn the main command dial. Both of these controls are located on top of the camera. When aperture-priority mode is enabled, you can do both of them. The camera must determine both the shutter speed and the ISO sensitivity.
  - ▪ Making use of manual exposure controls. When using manual exposure mode, the main command dial sets the shutter speed, which can range from 1/25 to 1/4000 of a second, while the sub-command dial sets the aperture. When the camera is in manual exposure mode, the aperture is set via the main command dial. To modify the sensitivity of the ISO setting, first push the ISO button and then turn the main command dial.
- o **Enable Video Recording**. If you want to start recording movies, turn the Photo/Movie switch to the Movie position.
- o **Select an AF-Area option and an Autofocus Mode** by using the AF/MF switch on the body to choose the best focus mode for you, whether it's autofocus or manual focus. Next, choose an AF-area mode and decide whether you want to use AF-S or AF-F for your focusing system.
- o **Change the Audio Level**: You can adjust the recording volume using the "Microphone Sensitivity" box in the Movie Shooting menu. You can select Manual Sensitivity, which allows you to adjust the level with an audiometer, or Auto Sensitivity, which allows the Z8 to determine the volume. If Auto Sensitivity is enabled, the Z8 will determine the volume level. If you need to make a quiet movie, you also have the option to turn off the sound recording so that it can

be added later during post-production along with voice-overs or other sounds.

- o **Start/stop recording**: Press the "movie recording" button with the red dot to begin recording and lock the focus. To stop recording, press the red dot button again. After that, the recording will be completed. The video is displayed on the LCD panel while it is being shot, and the frame rate is consistent. However, the viewfinder adds no information to the viewing area. Hit the DISP button while recording a video to control how much information is incorporated into the format.
- o **No Flash**: The electrical flash function cannot be used while recording video because it is currently turned off. If you have a Nikon SB-500 camera, you can use the camera's built-in LED movie light.

Trimming Your Movies

You can only edit the beginning or conclusion of a clip on camera, and it must be at least two seconds long. If you wish to make more complex modifications, you'll need video editing software that supports AVI files. These programs include tools for adding logos, special effects, and scene changes. There are hundreds of free video producers that you can find by searching Google for "AVI Editor." You can also put together many clips to make one movie. You can also adjust and cut video in the camera by using the Retouch menu or the Playback tool. **The process has not been changed in any way. In-camera cutting and editing can be done by doing the following:**

1. Start movie clip. If you press the Playback button, the photo review can begin. You can start playing a clip with the multi-selection center button once you've found one you want to change.

- • To make changes to a video clip, go to the Retouch menu and select "Edit video" while it is displayed on screen.

2. Start editing mode. You can skip the opening few seconds of a video by pausing it at the first frame you want to save and then hitting the down button to resume playback from that point forward. This removes the opening few seconds of the video. The movie progress bar, which can be found in the bottom left section of the screen, will display the part of the movie that you are presently watching at that time. When the movie is over, you can use the left and right buttons or the main or sub-command knobs to move through the frames while the video is stopping. The frames will then show up in the order that they were shot.

3. Trim. You should view the entire video until you find the final frame you wish to keep. Before cutting the video from the very end of the movie, use your remote control's down button to pause it. Turning the main command dial allows you to rapidly get to the index point that was saved in the following clip.

4. Pick a start or end point. While the video is halted, the "I" button will show the changing options. From there, select the "Select Start/End Point" option. You will be given the option of starting the animation from the current frame or the final frame. Please click OK again once you've made your choices.

5. Start playback again. To resume playing or return to where you left off after pausing, simply hit the multi-selector center button. Along with the primary control dial, which takes you to the next saved index point, there are buttons for Pause, Rewind, Advance, and Single Frame that allow you to navigate between different areas of your clip. You can utilize these controls in conjunction with the main control dial. Remember that the final segment of your video must be at least two seconds long. I appreciate that you paid attention to this small detail.

6. Check the trim. There will be a pop-up that asks you to continue. After you decide whether to say yes or no, click the OK button.

7. Save the video. There are four options available when it comes time to save the video after it has been shrunk in size:

- **Save As New File**." The main video file will be kept in a safe place, and a second copy of the edited clip will be kept on your computer in a different file.
- **Overwrite Existing File**. You no longer have the whole video that was saved on your memory card; you only have the section that you modified. Before you pick this option, you should be very careful, because it will stop you from getting the video back to its original, unmodified state.
- **Cancel**. Start the editing mode, and then come back to it later.
- **Preview**. Check out the version that has been modified. After that, you can choose to rename the file, save it as a new file, or end the process.

The Z8 will display a green progress bar and the words "Saving Movie" on the screen while it saves the cut clip to your memory card. To avoid missing a previously stored clip, do not interrupt the procedure, even if it takes some time. As a result, you should ensure that your camera's battery is completely charged before you begin editing a recording.

Saving a Frame

With the current video format's quality, you can save each frame of a movie as a JPEG still. Just follow the steps that were already given.

- Simply use the "**down**" button to pause the video at the desired frame.
- You can choose to **Save Selected Frame** from the menu that comes up when you press the "**i**" button.

- Use the up button to save an image of the selected frame.
- Once you have made your decision, click OK to confirm it.
- The memory card will store a photo of the frame you just captured.

CHAPTER FIFTEEN

IMAGE EDITING

Retouch and My Menus

After snapping a picture, you can alter it by selecting the Retouch option from the menu. When viewing a picture in Playback mode, press the "i" button to display the menu of options available during playback. To view your options, select Retouch and hit the right button on the multi selector.

They include:

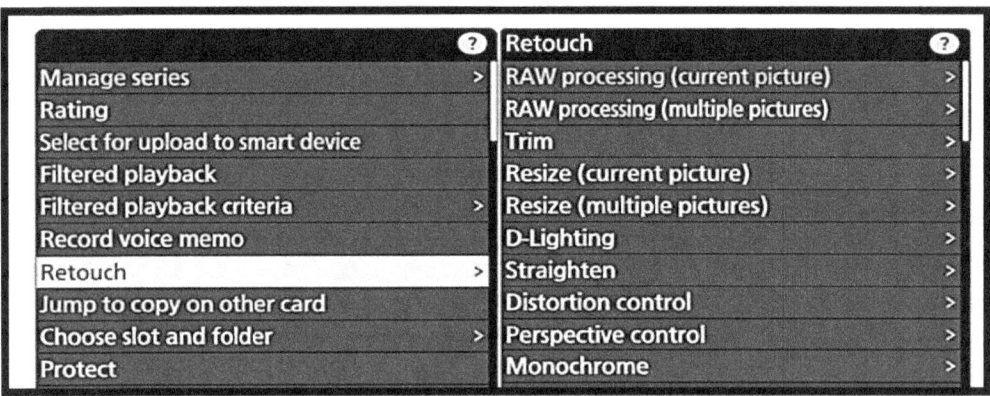

The Retouch menu is ideal for creating an altered copy of an image straight immediately, allowing you to print or email it without first importing it into your computer for more extensive editing. When you only shoot RAW images, you can utilize it to create a JPEG replica of the image in the camera. Except for copies created with the Image Overlay option, you can alter images that have previously been processed via the Retouch menu. If you utilize more than one edit option, you may notice a reduction in quality.

To retouch a photo:

1. Choose image retouching option. You can select the desired choice from the Retouch menu and then press the right button on the multi-selector. Note: If you select to work on a picture that was shot in both RAW and JPEG formats, you will only be allowed to edit the RAW version. Your camera may not be able to display or modify an image that was taken in a different mode and stored on your memory card.

2. Manipulate image. You can edit the copy by selecting the choices from the Retouch menu item and then pressing OK or Playback to reverse your changes. If the wait for the Menus timer in **Custom Setting c3: Power off Delay** expires, the camera will exit the menu screen, and any modifications that have not been saved may be lost. You may want to set Menus for a longer power-off pause.

3. View copy. If you do not select the RAW Processing, Trim, or Resize options while creating a duplicate, the changed JPEG image will be the same size and quality as the original. Any scaled or cropped NEF and TIFF images are saved as JPEG Fine files. During the review, copies that have been fixed up have a paintbrush sign put to the upper left corner of them. After using one of the Retouch menu items to fix up an image, you can use the majority of the other options on the altered copy (excluding those from Trim Movie). Any that are not open will appear in gray. However, it is usually not a good idea to touch up a copy that has already been touched up, because you will lose some image quality each time.

RAW Processing (Current Picture)/(Multiple Pictures)

Any RAW image can be converted to a JPEG file with the RAW Processing tool. This item not only allows you to create a JPEG from any RAW file in your camera, but it also allows you to change the image quality and size, as well as perform a variety of important adjustments such as white balance, exposure, and noise reduction. Nikon has two versions of the utility, one dubbed "**Current Picture**" that allows you to instantly create a JPEG from any image. One says "**Multiple Pictures**," and you may use it to give a bunch of RAW files the same parameters as the JPEG version.

Just follow these steps:

1. Choose RAW image(s).. If you select the (Current Picture) form, the image will be processed straight away. When you pick (Multiple Pictures), you will be directed to the regular Z8 image selection screen. Here, you can:

- ∞ **Choose pictures** by looking at thumbnails and clicking the Zoom In button to see individual thumbnails of NEF files full screen; or click the Zoom Out button to select or deselect a thumbnail. To be sure and leave, click OK.
- ∞ When you **choose Date**, you can choose which slot your RAW images are in and then choose from a list of all the times you took pictures with that card. To be sure and leave, press OK.
- ∞ To **choose Folder**, pick a card slot and a folder name. Then press OK to confirm and leave the menu.
- ∞ **Choose Destination**. Choose a memory card slot for your JPEG files, and then press the left button on the multi-selector to confirm and leave.

2. Select attributes. To alter these elements of the RAW image information for the JPEG copies of the photographs you selected, use the up and down arrow keys on the multi-selector in the RAW processing screen: You can select between Fine, Normal, and Basic image quality, as well as *versions of each. You can also select Large, Medium, and Small image sizes, White Balance, Exposure Compensation, Set Picture Control, High ISO Noise Reduction, Color Space, Vignette Control, D-Lighting, Diffraction Compensation, and (only for the Z8) Portrait Impression Balance.

3. Examine image. Press and hold the Zoom In button to momentarily magnify the image. When you push the DISP button, you can go from seeing the original image to seeing the processed image.

4. Change your mind? If you change your mind, press the Play button to leave the processing screen.

5. Execute. Once all of the settings are correct, pick EXE (which stands for "Execute") at the top of the list and click "OK." With the settings you've chosen, the camera will create a JPEG file for each of the photographs you've chosen, and when it's finished, the monitor will display an Image Saved message.

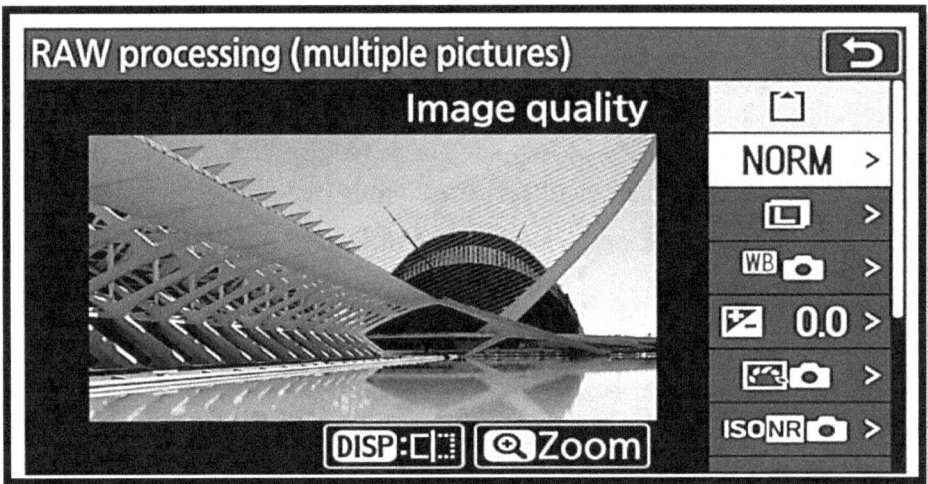

Trim

With this option, copies are created in certain sizes based on the end size you select. This function allows you to create smaller versions of images for emailing without first saving them to your computer.

Simply do these things:

o **Select your photo**. Go to the Retouch menu and select Trim while you are in Playback mode.

117

o **Choose your aspect ratio.** To change between 3:2, 4:3, 5:4, 16:9 (and their inverses), and 1:1 aspect ratios, turn the main command dial. The most frequent print sizes are 4 by 6 inches (3:2) and 8 by 10 inches (5:4), hence these proportions.

o **Crop in on your photo.** You can crop your image by using the Zoom In and Zoom Out buttons. As you zoom in, the upper-left corner displays the pixel measurements of the clipped image at the selected sizes. The trim sizes vary depending on the chosen Aspect Ratio and Image Size. The current size of the frame is displayed in yellow.

o **Move cropped area within the image.** You can move the yellow cutting line inside the frame by pressing the left/right and up/down buttons on the multi-selector.

o **Save the cropped image.** You can either press OK to save a copy of the image with the current crop and size, or press Play to exit the program without generating a copy. The Image Quality setting on copies created from JPEG Fine, Normal, or Standard is identical to the original. Copies produced from RAW files or with any RAW+JPEG configuration will utilize JPEG Fine compression. Remember that once an image has been saved, you may not be able to zoom in on it while it is playing back.

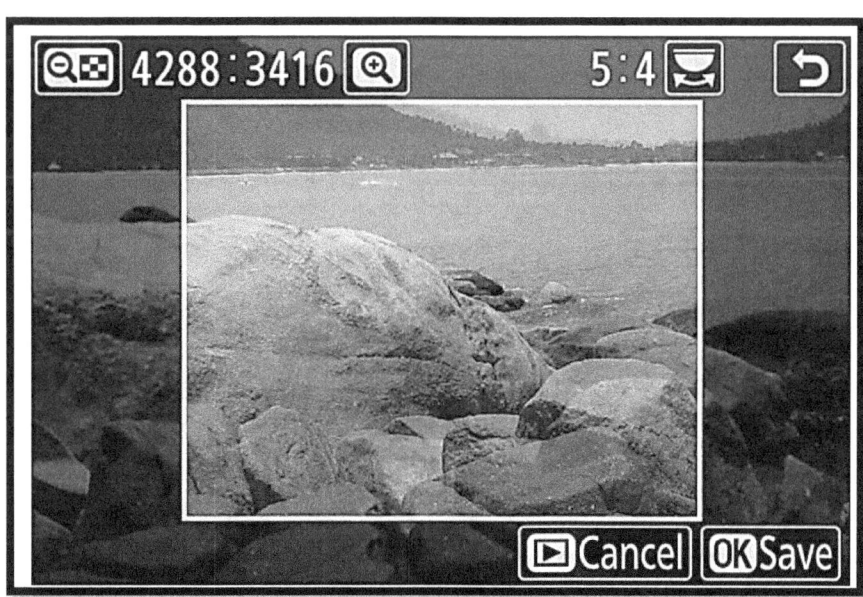

Resize (Current Picture)/(Multiple Pictures)

There are two additional options for changing the current picture or selecting several photos. It can be used when viewing a single image in full-size mode (by pressing the i button) or from the Retouch menu (which is useful for selecting and editing many images at once). To publish it on a website or send it by email, you may prefer smaller images.

Just do these things:

1. **Select Pictures**. From the Retouch menu, select one or more photos.

2. **Choose destination**. Pick the memory card slot with the image(s).

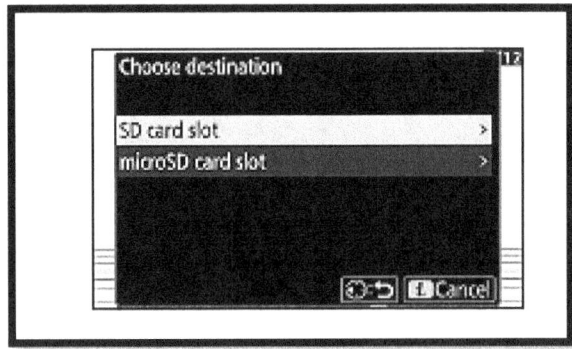

3. **Choose size**. Next, choose the copy's size from 2304 × 1536 (3.5 MB), 1920 × 1280 (2.5 MB), 1280 × 856 (1.1 MB), or 960 × 640 (0.6 MB).

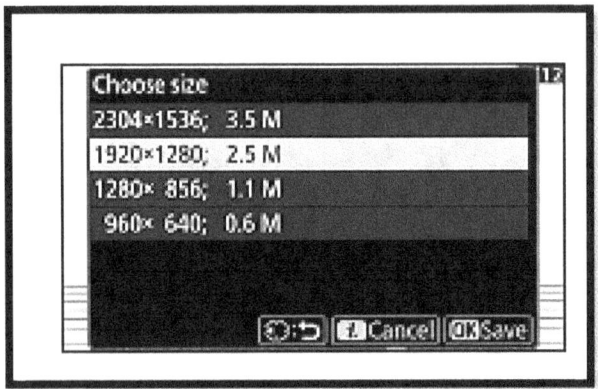

4. **Confirm**. To make a copy, select OK. To stop, hit the "i" button. To leave the Size screen, use the "left" arrow key. Keep in mind that, as with Trim, you may not be able to zoom in on a resized image when it is being played back after it has been saved.

D-Lighting

D-Lighting is Nikon's shade enhancement processing that occurs after an image has been captured. This differs from Active D-Lighting, which occurs as the photograph is taken. In other words, this option brightens the shadows in photographs as you gaze at them. After selecting your photo for change, use the up/down moving controls on the multi-selector to select High, Normal, or Low adjustments. Pressing the Zoom In button will increase the size of the image. The DISP button allows you to transition between the original version and the version you altered. When you're satisfied with the difference between the new image on the right and the old one on the left, click OK to save the copy to your memory card.

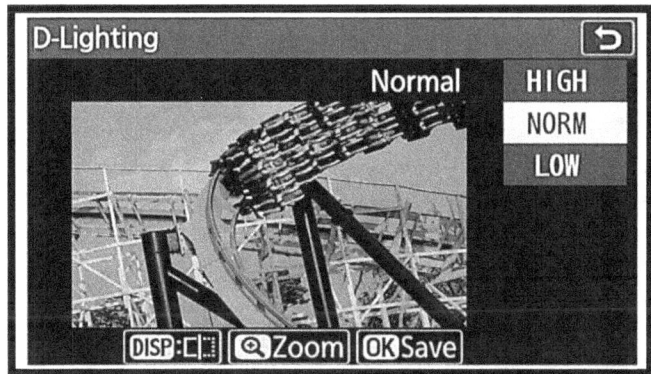

Straighten

You can use this to correct a crooked image by rotating it by up to five degrees in any direction, in quarter-degree increments from -20 to +20. To turn clockwise, hit the down button. To turn counterclockwise, hit the up button. The display will show you how much you need to repair. To transition between the original and fixed forms, zoom in on the image or click the DISP button. Press OK to make a fresh, correct copy. To exit the program without creating a copy, press the Play button. To create a square image, the camera must trim the borders of the rotated image, which means you will lose some picture information.

Distortion Control

When you select this option, the duplicate will have less barrel distortion (a falling-out effect) and pincushion distortion (an inward-bending effect). Both types of peripheral distortion are most visible near a picture's edges. When the camera detects distortion, you can select "**Auto**" to have it correct itself. As long as you have the manual, you can fix it yourself. Pressing the down arrow button reduces barrel distortion, which causes lines to bend outward at the borders. Pressing the up-arrow button reduces pincushion distortion, which causes lines to bow inward. In either case, some of the photo's margins will be removed from your image. The DISP button allows you to transition between the original and fixed form. Press OK to make a fresh, correct copy. To exit the program without creating a copy, press the Play button. When you use the Auto Distortion Control tool in the Photo Shooting menu to expose an image, you cannot utilize Auto.

Perspective Control

The falling-back effect generated by turning the camera to the top of a tall subject, such as a building, or to one side to acquire a longer structure or item, can be decreased by using this option to modify an image's perspective. Choose the direction you want to correct (refer to the left image below). You can correct the distortion by "tilting" the image in various directions with the up and down multi-selector buttons. (See the right image below) Press the DISP button to flip between the original image and the modified image, or you can zoom in on the image.

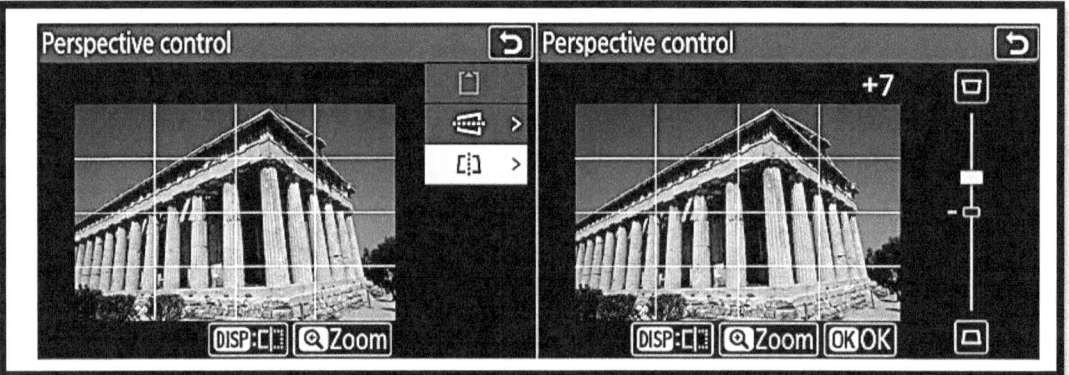

Monochrome

This Repair option allows you to create a copy of the chosen image in black-and-white, sepia-toned, or cyanotype (blue-and-white) format. To fine-tune the color saturation of the preview Sepia or Cyanotype version, press the up button on the multi-selector to make the colors richer, and the down button to make the colors less saturated. When you're satisfied with the adjustments, click OK to create a monochromatic clone. It will be given a title. To stop the playback, press the Play button. Always, the DISP button allows you to flip between the source image and the processed version.

Overlay (Add)

Because the layers are made with RAW data, this function lets you combine two RAW pictures (but only RAW files can be used) into a single image that Nikon says is better than a "double exposure" made in an image editor.

These steps will help you make this combined image:

- **Pick pictures**. To mark or unmark pictures, select two photos from the main selection screen and then use the Zoom Out button. To continue, press OK.
- **Fix the balance**. You can adjust the percentage of each image that will be utilized in the final edition by hitting the up and down buttons on the multi-selector. The standard percentage is 50/50, however you can modify it to any other amount you choose. The "up" button makes the first photo you select stronger, while the "down" button makes the second picture stronger.
- To save your merged copy, use the OK button. For your evaluation, the combined image is displayed in full frame and stored in the memory card in JPEG * format.

Lighten/Darken

You can't use these two options to make a single picture darker or lighter. Instead, they are used to join the photos in a way similar to Photoshop. The camera measures the pixels in each picture and only uses the best or darkest one for the final version.

Motion Blend

This option allows you to select a group of RAW (NEF) photographs in a row, locate moving subjects, and combine them into a single JPEG image. You can select from 5 photographs (the smallest) and 20 pictures (the largest). To finish editing, press OK. While this feature is enabled, the background must remain the same in all photographs, and the subject must move.

Using My Menu

Recent Settings and My Menu are the two different names for the last menu on the main menu screen. Recent Settings is the usual mode. It just shows a list of the 20 menu items you used most recently, which changes all the time. You may find it easier to enable the "My Menu" option instead. This will only display the menu items you added from the "**Playback,**" "**Photo Shooting,**" "**Video Recording,**" "**Custom Settings,**" "**Setup,**" **and "Retouch"** options, based on which ones you use the most. Keep in mind that when you push the MENU button, the camera returns to the previous menu and text you viewed. So, you may design My Menu to contain only the most-used items, and if you haven't already used another menu, tapping the MENU button will take you directly to those items.

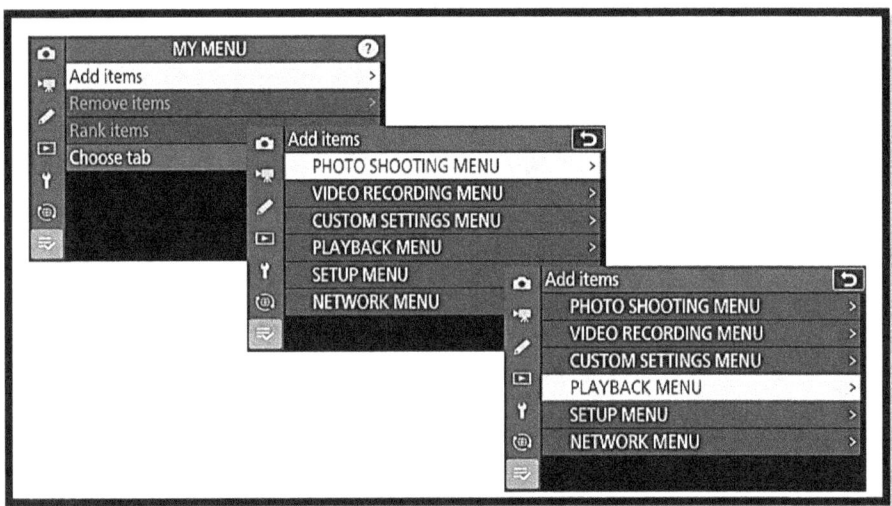

It's simple to switch between them. There is a menu option called **Choose Tab** in both the My Menu and the Recent Settings windows. If you pick that item and press the right multi-selector button, you'll see a screen that lets you choose between the My Menu and the Recent Settings menu. To confirm, press **OK**. I normally include options in My Menu that I use frequently but are not available via straight buttons. I utilize settings like High ISO NR, Long Exp. NR, and Battery Info since I may want to toggle noise reduction on or off or check how my battery is performing while shooting. I do not adjust ISO or WB in My Menu, even if I can do so through the menu system because I can do it rapidly by tapping appropriate buttons and turning the main and sub-command knobs. You can always add or remove items from My Menu and rearrange the items so that the ones you use most often are at the top of the list. **To use My Menu, read this whole page. To put entries on My Menu:**

1. Go to the "**My Menu**" and pick "**Add Items**."
2. A menu list will be displayed, including ones for taking pictures, recording videos, customizing settings, playing back videos, setting up the camera, and connecting to a network. Pick one and click the right button on the multi-selector.

3. Choose the menu item you want to add from the ones that are already there and press **OK**.
4. At the top of the **My Menu** screen, you'll find the words "**Choose Position**." You can select a number from the list by clicking the **up and down** buttons. Then, press **OK** to confirm and add the new item.
5. Do step **1–4** again if you want to add more items to **My Menu**.

To change the order of the menu items, do the following:

1. Pick **Rank Items** from the My Menu screen.
2. Pick out the thing you want to move with the up and down buttons, then press **OK**.
3. Move the thing you've chosen by pressing the up and down buttons, then press **OK**.
4. Do steps 2–3 again to move more items.

When an item is marked in the My Menu screen, you can press the Trash button to get rid of it from the list. Steps to get rid of various items:

o From the "**My Menu**" page, click "**Remove Items**."
o A collection of menu options appears, each with a checkmark. To delete an item, scroll down and click the right button on the multi-selector. This will indicate its box. If you change your mind, simply pick the item you wish to remove and press the right button again.
o When you're finished, click the OK button and choose "Done."
o Select OK to save the changes.

CHAPTER SIXTEEN
THE PLAYBACK MENU

The blue-coded Playback menu, which contains 12 items, allows you to select options for displaying, reviewing, transferring, and copying photographs you've taken. The graphic below shows the first seven entries. Keep in mind that some items, such as Delete, are functions rather than settings, therefore there is no default value.

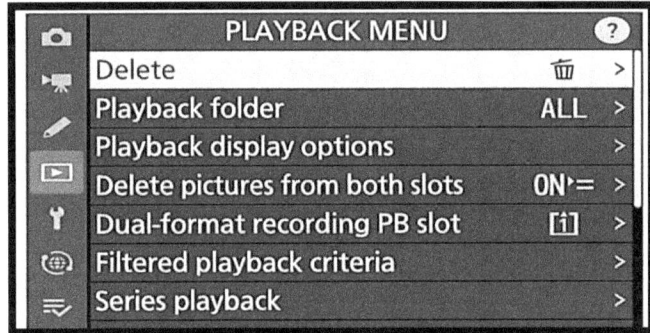

Delete

Pick this menu item, and you'll find four options: Selected Pictures (to pick which photos to rate); Candidates for Deletion (to get rid of photos marked as "delete"); Pictures Shot on Selected Dates (to get rid of all photos taken on a specific day); or All Pictures.

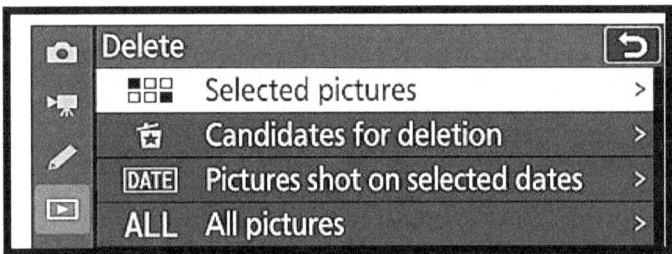

Choose an image by using one of these options:

- **Selected Pictures**. A selection screen, similar to the one shown below. The horizontal buttons on the multi-selector can be used to go through the various views of the images displayed. If you hold down the Zoom In button, the marked image will expand until it fills the entire screen. To remove a highlighted image, use the Zoom Out button. To erase a previously marked image, use the

Zoom Out button. When an image is designated for deletion, a yellow cross appears in the upper right corner of the picture. When you've finished writing, press OK to delete. If you want to stop, click "**No**" on the screen that appears.

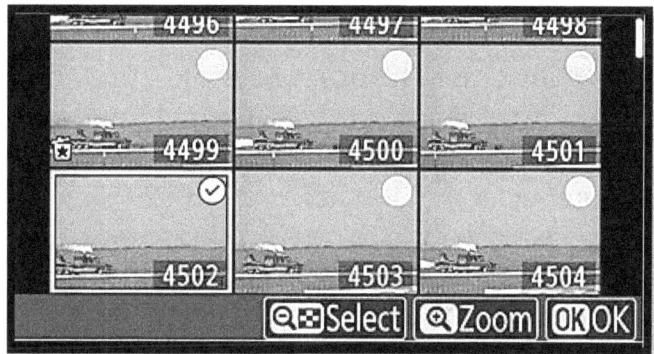

- **Candidates for Deletion**. The Rating option in the Playback version of the i menu allows you to mark photos for deletion. This option deletes the photographs. This is where you can't select photographs. Instead, while in Playback mode, hit the "i" button and then select "**Rating**" from the resulting screen (left). Next, spin the main command dial and click the trash can button (right).

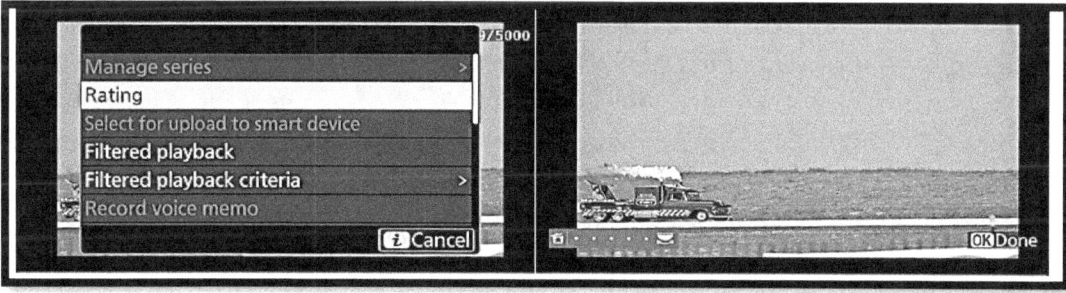

- **Pictures Shot on Selected Dates**. There is a list of the times the photos were taken. To mark a date as chosen or to remove a mark from an already marked date, hit the appropriate multi-selector button. If you are certain you want to erase all images, click the Zoom Out button to confirm. After selecting one or more dates, hit OK to allow the camera to proceed to the confirmation page.
- **All Pictures**. Pick a Slot, press **OK**, and then choose Yes or No to delete the pictures.
  - This menu will not erase photographs identified with an overlaid key icon and protected with the Protect option from the i menu during Playback. Using Format is usually considerably faster than selecting Delete: All

Pictures and is also a superior way to reset your memory card to a brand-new, blank state. Remember that deleting images in this manner takes longer than erasing the entire card with the Format command.

Playback Folder

To save the photos that your camera takes, it will create folders on your memory card. The first folder is assigned a number, such as 100NCZ_8, and when it is filled, a new folder with a higher number is created instantly. When a folder contains 5,000 images or a picture with the number 9999, it is considered full. If you use the same memory card, the second camera will create its folder. As a result, you may end up with many folders on the same memory card until you format it and start creating folders all over again. When using the Playback feature to display pictures, this menu item lets you select which folders are used.

Here are the options you have:

- **NCZ_8**. The camera will only use the folders it creates on your memory card; folders created by other cameras will not be utilized. All of the camera's groups' photos will be displayed. This is the folder's name by default. You can change the names of these folders by going to the Photo Shooting menu and selecting Storage Folder > Rename.
- **All (the default).** Regardless of the camera that took the image, all folders containing photos that the camera can read will be available. If you frequently exchange memory cards between cameras and want to review each photo, this setting may be useful. This is especially critical if you plan to format the memory card. If the photos match the Design Rule for Camera File System (DCF) requirements, you will be able to see them even if they were taken with a non-Nikon camera.
- **Current**. The camera will only display photographs from the current folder. For example, if you've been shooting a lot at an event and have more than 5,000 photos in one folder (or an image with the number 9999), and the camera has created a new folder to accommodate the overflow, you can use this setting to only see the most recent photos in the current folder. The Active Folder option in the Photo Shooting menu allows you to swap from the current folder to any other folder on your memory card.

Playback Display Options

This menu item can help you reduce or increase the clutter on the Playback screen by allowing you to select which information and displays are presented. To enable or disable an information item, scroll to it and use the right multi-selector button to check the box next to it. If you want to unmark a previously checked item, press the correct button. If no boxes are ticked, the default view is the image with the basic information at the bottom of the screen. When shooting data, you could need more than one page. You can scroll through them by using the up and down buttons on the multi-selector.

Your options for more information are:
1. **Focus Point**:
   - **Description**: Displays the active focus point(s) with red high-contrast lighting.
   - **Usage**: Select this option to easily identify the active focus point(s) during shooting, ensuring precise focusing.
2. **Mark First Shot in Series**:
   - **Description**: Adds a label to the first image taken in a continuous shooting series.
   - **Usage**: When reviewing photos, an icon of a stack of pictures and the number of shots in the series will appear in the top right corner of the first picture, making it easy to identify the start of a burst sequence.
3. **Exposure Info**:
   - **Description**: Displays only the frame number and basic exposure information such as ISO sensitivity, release mode, shutter speed, aperture, and exposure correction.
   - **Usage**: Enables quick access to essential exposure details, helping you assess and adjust your settings efficiently.
4. **Highlights**:
   - **Description**: Blinks with a black edge during picture review to indicate overexposed parts of your image.
   - **Usage**: Use this feature to identify areas of overexposure. If necessary, apply exposure compensation to reduce the exposure and preserve important details. Avoid settings that might cause desired dark details to disappear.
5. **RGB Histogram**:
   - **Description**: Displays both luminance (brightness) and RGB histograms.
   - **Usage**: Utilize the up/down multi-display selector buttons to adjust the histogram view. This feature helps you analyze the brightness and color distribution in your image, allowing for precise exposure and color adjustments.

These display settings enhance your ability to monitor and adjust critical aspects of your photography, leading to better control and improved results.

Delete Pictures from Both Slots

If you erase photographs by utilizing the Playback menu item, this entry gives you the option to decide whether or not to keep additional duplicates of an image. Your camera can store numerous copies of the same image in many different locations, and this capability is determined by the purpose that you select for the second card space. Since there will only be one duplicate of each photo, this entry does not matter if you have configured the second place to be an Overflow destination when the first card is full. Leaving things as it is is the best option if you do not wish to make any changes. If you choose to delete an image, the camera will notify you that a copy of the image is stored on the second card and will then request permission to delete the image. If you select "Yes," the instance will be removed immediately. If you select "No," it will be stored as a backup if you change your mind or make a serious error.

Dual-Format Recording PB Slot

It has two slots for memory cards. The Z8 has two slots: one for CFexpress/XQD cards and one for SD cards. The Z8's Photo Shooting menu has options for Primary Slot Selection and Secondary Slot Selection. You can choose one of these two slots as the primary slot and the other as the secondary slot. The Z8 has two slots, each of which may accept a different type of memory card. You can control how each slot's memory card is used. When the first slot card is full, instruct the camera to use the second slot as an additional. You can also instruct it to copy each shot to both slots as a backup or to save RAW photographs on one card and JPEGs on the other. This input only applies if you shoot in RAW+JPEG format and select RAW Primary—JPEG Secondary in the Z8's Secondary Slot Function entry. This input determines which of your dual-format photos should be displayed during playback. Depending on your preference, you can view either the version stored in the CFexpress/XQD slot or the version saved in the SD card slot (on the Z8).

Filtered Playback Criteria

Normally, when you play back an image, your camera displays all of the photos in the active folder. You can sort through your photos and display only those that suit your criteria by selecting from some categories. A white line surrounds the image to indicate that it is only being presented filtered. Along with this menu item, the Playback version of the i menu allows you to select playback and specify parameters for limited playback. This entry specifies the filters that will be used when you start limited playback.

The filters that can be used are:
- **Protected images**. You must protect each image on its own or in a group.
- **Picture Type**. You can choose photos or videos.
- **Rating**. You can choose any number of stars between 0 and 5, as well as pictures that have been marked for deletion.
- **Uploads**. You can look at the ones you picked to save to your computer. In the Playback part of the i menu, you can pick which pictures to send. You can look at pictures that have already been uploaded to a computer or FTP site, photos that have not been uploaded yet, or both.
- **Voice memo**. Use the Playback option of the i menu to see pictures that have been marked with a recorded voice message. The i menu can be used to listen to voice memos while reviewing.
- **Retouched pictures**. Using the Playback option of the i menu, look over every image that has been edited.

When you choose any mix of the factors mentioned, you can do things like look at only protected still photos that have four or five stars, if that's what you want. As long as you've protected or rated the pictures, this is a quick and easy way to sort through a lot of them. **Simply follow these steps to conduct an image search using the categories you've chosen:**
1. Press the Playback button to display an image.
2. Press the i button to display the i menu.
3. Select Filtered Playback from the menu.
4. Press OK to display the filtered images.

Series Playback

During playback, this entry gives you some tools that can help you look over pictures. Pick one of these three options:
- **Sub-selector Displays First Shot**. Pressing the sub-selector joystick left or right will take you to the first shot in each continuous series. This setting is enabled by default. Use the directional pad's left and right buttons to travel forward or backward one frame at a time. If you disable this setting, the directional pad buttons and sub-selector buttons will only travel one frame at a time.
- **Auto Series Playback**. After finishing a continuous series, you can start a manual image evaluation. This parameter is turned off by default. Turn this option on if you want the camera to immediately display the individual shots in order. After you hit Playback to view the first image in a series, the camera will begin presenting the other photographs one by one after around three seconds.

- **List Series as a Single Thumbnail**. Help yourself out by turning on this option. Using photos will make it easier to find a specific scene or series. When this option is enabled, just the first shot in a continuous sequence is given as a picture with a "stack" background to show that there are other photographs in the series.

Picture Review

Sometimes it's useful to have the image you just shot appear on the shooting monitor right away so you can look at it. If your most recent image is fine, you may be adjusting the exposure or focusing. You can also feel nervous and want to make sure you took a picture. Picture review has saved my bacon several times when I made a terrible setting by mistake, such as setting ISO 25600 when it wasn't needed or requested.

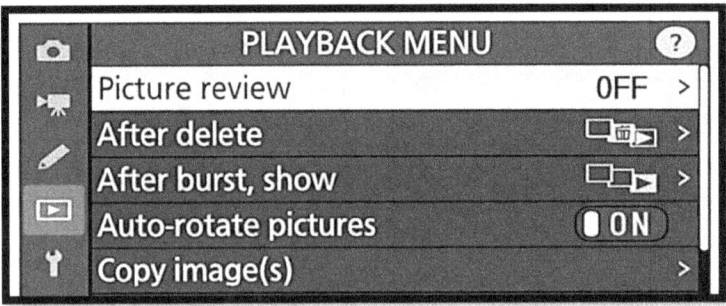

If you want to save battery life (the LCD panel and EVF are two of the greatest power consumers), speed up, or make things easier, you should usually avoid having the camera automatically evaluate your images. If you just snapped eight pictures in succession during a football game, do you need to view every frame on the screen as the camera clears its buffer and uploads the images to your memory card? You can select the mode to utilize with this menu item. You can specify whether the review image should appear always, solely on the LCD monitor, or never. Nikon did not provide us with an "On (Viewfinder Only)" option for examining photographs, but I will show you a couple of ways to get around it.
- **On**. Your shot will show in the viewfinder or on the LCD monitor, based on which device you are using. Image review is automatic after every shot is taken.
- **On (Only Monitor).** To see the image review, move the camera away from your eye. Image review is only presented on the rear panel LCD monitor if you are not looking through the viewfinder.
- **Off**. When you press the Playback button, images will only display. Nikon was smart and set this as the usual setting.

After Delete

When you've eliminated an image, you'll probably want to do one of three things: show the next image (in the order shot), show the prior image, or show both the next and previous images, depending on the direction you were traveling throughout the image review. **You can select from the following:**

- **Show Next**. Because Nikon thinks you'll want to look at the picture that was taken after the one you just deleted, this is what it does by default.
- **Show Previous**. When I'm shooting sports with the continuous setting, I use this setting frequently. After capturing the images in a series, I press the Playback button to view the final one. Sometimes I think the entire series missed the boat. When I want to delete an image, I sometimes press the Trash button twice. Then I go back and remove the five, six, or eleven other images that were in the way. You'll regularly find yourself with extra time at football games and wish to remove a lousy set of photos to save time studying them on the internet and making some space on your card.
- **Continue as Before**. This option makes sense: if you were scrolling backward or forward and removing pictures as you went, you might want to keep going in the same way and get rid of the bad ones. You can tell your camera to act in that way by using this setting.

After Burst, Show

When Image Review is switched off, this menu option allows you to select which image to show after a shot. In actuality, the camera will not display any images on the LCD monitor while you are shooting a burst, allowing it to record shots and save them on your memory card at maximum speed. When the burst ends, one image, either the first in the sequence or the last captured, will be displayed on the screen. I prefer to look at the final image. If the exposure and focus are fine, I can presume the rest of the set is good as well and start another burst right away if necessary. Instead, choose First Picture in Burst if you want to see the first photo and then possibly continue looking at the rest.

Auto-rotate Pictures

When you use the camera to photograph vertical subjects in portrait (tall) mode rather than landscape (wide), you don't want to see the shots tilted to the side on the monitor and viewfinder, or in your computer's photo viewing and editing software. The camera includes a motion sensor that can detect whether a photo was taken while it was rotated and hide that information in the image format. There are two ways to apply

132

the direction information. If this option is enabled, the camera will automatically rotate photographs displayed on the monitor and in the viewfinder. If you disable this option, you can ignore the data and view the photographs without being rotated (you must turn the camera to see them in the correct direction). As previously stated, the embedded file data can be used by your image editor to rotate images on your computer screen immediately. This menu setting only controls whether the image is turned when displayed on the camera's LCD or in the electronic viewfinder. Spin Tall is an option that disables the camera's ability to spin images taken in a vertical position. If you disable this option, your image-editing program will still be able to read the stored rotation data and display your images properly. The image seems large on your monitor, but you must turn the camera around to see it well. When you enable Spin Tall, the camera will rotate images taken in portrait mode on the monitor screen so you don't have to turn the camera to see them. This direction causes the image presented (but not the display itself) to shrink in size, implying that the longest dimension of the monitor is shown using the smallest dimension of the display. Do not turn your camera to view vertical images in their natural orientation. If you don't mind a smaller image, toggle this feature on. If, like me, you like a larger image and are ready to use the camera, switch this option off. To see the largest review image on the display, turning the camera is not a big deal and is worth the effort.

Copy Image(s)

When a camera has two slots, one of my favorite features is the ability to use two memory cards at the same time. Making backup photographs on two cards is one of the best things you can do while you're moving or any other time when you can't access your computer.

Here are some examples of what I do:

- **Shoot to two cards simultaneously.** You can use this as a backup right away in case the pictures on your main card get damaged or lost. The recommended size for your two cards is equal.
- **Make a copy.** Use the Copy Image(s) feature to transfer an image from one card to another. When taking images, use only one card and make a backup onto a second card at the end of the day instead of shooting on two cards at once, which slows down the camera slightly. You can copy all or a few of the photos you've taken.
- **Leave your laptop or external storage at home.** Now that I use Nikon cameras with two memory card spots instead of my hard drive or laptop with a built-in reader, I leave them at home more often. Making copies in the camera is easy

for me when I'm only going to be gone for a day or two. I don't need to deal with an extra device.

Just follow these instructions (which are only available when two memory cards are present in the camera) to move an image from one card to another:

1. **Access copy menus**. From the Playback menu, pick **Copy Images(s)**. Select **Source, Select Picture(s), Select Destination Folder, and Copy Picture(s)?** are the four options you may have. In the image below, they are at the upper left.

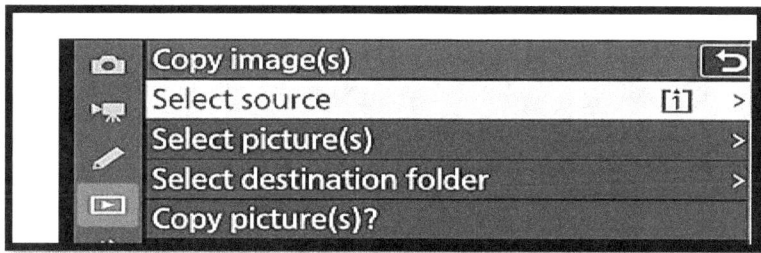

- If there are images on only one card, all other options will be grayed out, and the card with the pictures will be chosen automatically.
- You can choose Select Source to choose which card spot to copy from if there are already pictures on both cards.
- All four options will be offered if you have already marked some pictures.

2. **Select Source**. Pick Source and press the right button on the multi-selector to choose photos from the non-default spot that is already chosen. This works if you have pictures on both cards. Pick the slot you want, then press the right button again to go back to the before menu.

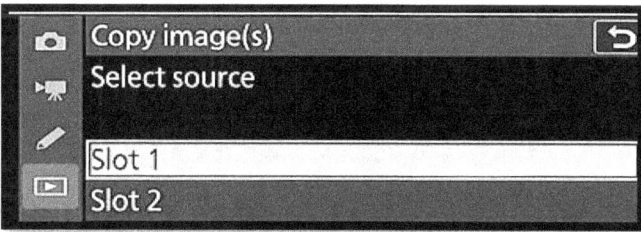

3. **Select Pictures**. Select the picture(s) you want to use and press the right button. A screen shows up. Now you can pick from:
- **All Pictures in Slot**. You will be taken back to the previous menu if you choose this, and all of the pictures on the card will be chosen.
- **Images in a folder in that slot**. If there are multiple folders on the card, they will all be displayed. The screen in the middle right of the image below appears

when you select a folder and press the appropriate button. You can now select either **Select All Pictures or Select Protected Pictures**, as you previously indicated. If you pick Deselect All at the top of the list, any previously selected images will be unselected immediately. This takes you to the Deselect All/Select screen, where you can highlight photographs and clear them by clicking the OK button.

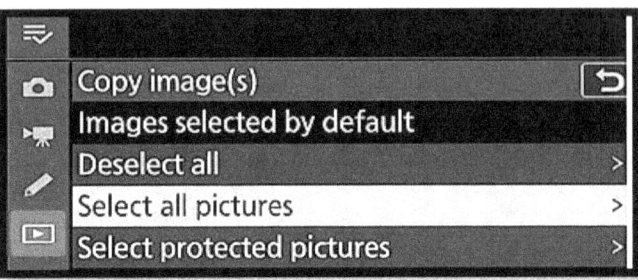

- **Select destination folder**. When you've finished selecting photographs, press OK to return to the Copy Image(s) screen. You can click Select Destination Folder and select a folder on the target card by number or from an existing list of folders. You do not need to designate a folder for the destination; the camera will create one on the memory card for you.
- **Start copying**. Choice of a destination. If you do not want to, select Copy Picture(s). The amount of pictures to be copied will be presented on the acceptance screen. If you choose "**Yes**" and press "**OK**," a screen with a green progress bar will appear while the copying is taking place. When the job is completed, you will get a notification stating "Copy Complete." To exit the menus, hit OK, then the MENU button twice. You may simply press the shutter release button.

CHAPTER SEVENTEEN

ELECTRONIC FLASH WITH THE NIKON Z8

Electronic flash lighting is created by driving photons generated by an electrical charge that accumulates in a capacitor through a glass tube holding xenon gas, which absorbs the energy and produces the flash of light. When the camera is set to automated mode (also known as Nikon iTTL), the main flash is preceded by one or more mini-bursts. This enables the Z8 to detect how much light is bouncing off your subject and backdrop and to communicate with **other wirelessly connected external flash units. In use, the Z8 can be coupled to external strobes in several ways, including:**

- **Camera mounted/hardwired external dedicated flash**. Nikon SC-28/SC-29 cables or the accessory "hot" shoe on top of the camera can be used to wirelessly connect units offered by Nikon or other suppliers that are compatible with Nikon's Creative Lighting System (CLS).

- **Wireless dedicated flash**. Using pre-flash signals, a CLS-compatible device may be engaged before the principal flash burst, allowing two-way communication between the camera and flash unit. The triggering flash can either be a wireless non-flashing attachment like the Nikon SU-800, which just "speaks" to the external flashes or a CLS-compatible flash unit in Master Mode.

- **Wired, non-intelligent mode**. The Nikon AS-15 Sync Terminal converter, which can be put in the hot shoe on top of the camera, makes it simple to add a PC/X connection to the Z8. A linked flash is instructed to fire using the PC/X connection, a simple camera/flash interface that simply delivers one piece of information in one direction. There is no other way to communicate between the camera and the flash. The Nikon Z8's PC/X connection may be used to connect non-dedicated/non-CLS-friendly flash units, manual non-CLS flash, flash equipment from other manufacturers that can utilize a PC cable and even Nikon-branded speedlights that you choose to use with the Z8 in a non-CLS, "unintelligent" mode.

- **Radio/Infrared transmitter/receivers**. A specific radio-compatible flash unit called the Nikon SB-5000 may be used to link flash units to the Z8. Additionally, you can utilize a wireless infrared or radio transmitter that is an add-on, such as the Pocket Wizard, Radio Popper, or Godox X wireless system.

They commonly attach to the Z8's accessory shoe, and if the Z8 instructs the hot shoe to fire, they transmit a signal. The camera and flash have no additional connection in the most basic of these devices, which just function as a wireless PC/X connector (apart from the firing instruction). More advanced units, on the other hand, include inbuilt controllers and may send extra instructions to receivers when linked to the appropriate flash units. I use one to avoid switching the power output from the camera to my Alien Bees studio flash.

- **Simple slave connection**. Before advanced wireless communication, off-camera, non-wired flash devices were routinely activated via a slave device. These triggers, which can be tiny external ones or incorporated into the remote flash, fire when the slave's optical sensor recognizes a burst launched by the camera. When the slave flash "sees" the primary flash, it activates soon enough to contribute to the same exposure.

The main issue with this type of connection, aside from the absence of cognitive communication between the camera and the flash, is that the slave may be deceived by any pre-flashes emitted by the other strobes and fire too soon. A specific "digital" mode found on more contemporary slave triggers only fires from the main flash burst and ignores the pre-flash.

The Moment of Exposure

The Z8's vertically moveable shutter consists of two curtains. Just before the flash fires, the front (first) curtain rises and advances to the other side of the frame while the shutter is fully open. The flash might then be activated (referred to as front-curtain sync), resulting in flash exposure. After a delay of 30 seconds to 1/200th of a second (or faster when high-speed sync is utilized), a rear (second) curtain moves along the sensor plane and re-covers it. If the flash is shot just as the back curtain is about to close, rear-curtain sync is activated. However, the highest shutter speed that may be utilized to take a shot in either case is 1/200th second, unless you're utilizing the high-speed 1/200th (Auto FP) sync option.

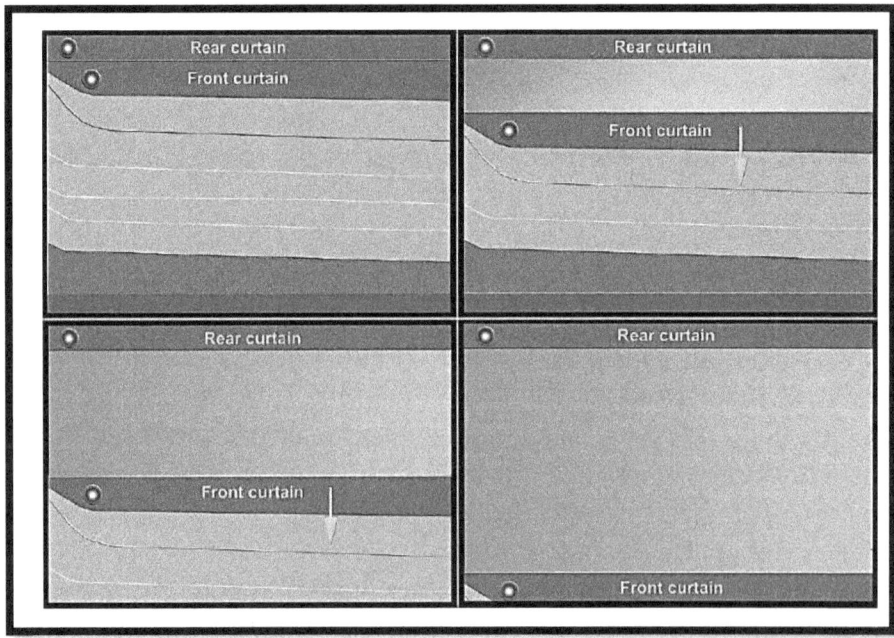

The hypothetical illustration of a generic shutter in the image above demonstrates how this works; your Z8's shutter does not resemble this. Both curtains are pulled firmly in the top left corner. Right near the top, the front curtain begins to lower, showing a tiny slit that leads to the sensor hidden behind the shutter. The front curtain gradually lowers from the bottom left to the lower right in the illustration, until the sensor is fully displayed. Here is a closer look at what occurs when a photo is taken in a matter of milliseconds using an electric flash.

The following list assumes you are operating in iTTL exposure mode.

1. **Flash Sync mode**. After selecting a shooting mode, pick the flash sync option that appears. Pressing the I button will display the Flash Mode option in the Photo Shooting Menu, which is the third choice from the left in the top row if your I menu has not been changed. If you often move between flash sync modes, you may designate a button in Custom Setting f2: Custom Control Assignment to trigger the adjustment.

2. **Metering method**. Pick the metering method you choose from the matrix, center-weighted, spot, or highlight-weighted options.

3. **Metering method**. Install the external flash and activate it (or connect it via wire). A ready light displays in the viewfinder and on the rear of the dedicated flash when the camera is ready to shoot a shot (however the flash may not be completely charged when the light initially appears).

4. **Verify exposure**. Pick a shutter speed when using the Manual, Program, or Shutter-priority exposure modes; select an aperture when using the Aperture-priority and Manual exposure modes.

5. **Preview Lighting**. To preview the lighting effect, assign the Preview behavior to a button (the conventional options are Fn1 or Fn2). By hitting that button, a modeling flash burst can be produced.

6. **Lock flash setting (if desired)**. If the primary subject is substantially off-center, you can frame the shot with the main topic in the center, lock the flash to the exposure required to light that subject, and then reframe with the desired composition. To lock the flash level, hit the Flash Value (FV) Lock button (many users use Custom Settings f2 to assign the Fn1 or Fn 2 buttons for this purpose). When you press the FV lock button, the flash will emit a monitor pre-flash to identify the right flash level before locking at that level until you press the FV lock button again to open it. FV lock icons are present in both the viewfinder and the monochrome control panel.

7. **Get a picture**. Press the shutter release all the way.

8. **Z8 receives distance data**. With the FTZ adaptor attached, the Z8 can now receive focus distance from Z-mount lenses as well as F-mount E, D, or G-series lenses.

9. **Pre-flash emitted**. The external flash shoots many pre-flash bursts. In Commander Mode, one burst set may be used to control additional wireless flash units, while another can be used to set exposure. Pre-flashes seldom register because they occur so quickly before the major flash.

138

10. **Exposure calculated**. The sensor detects pre-flash once the signal has bounced and returned. It computes the image's brightness and contrast to determine exposure. When employing Matrix metering, the Z8 scans the scene to decide whether the subject should be backlit (for fill flash), whether the subject requires more ambient light exposure to balance the scene with the flash exposure, or if the situation should be classified in another way. The topic is located inside the frame using the camera-to-subject information and the intensity with which the subject is focused. If spot metering is selected, only conventional i-TTL (without balanced fill flash) is utilized.
11. **Front curtain opens**. Ambient light exposure begins when the actual shutter curtain is entirely open.
12. **Flash fired**. Depending on whether front or back sync is utilized, the camera sends a signal to one or more flashes to initiate flash discharge at the appropriate triggering time. The flash is quenched as soon as the required exposure is met.
13. **Shutter closes**. The live view of the sensor continues when the shutter closes. You're ready to take a fresh photo. Don't forget to press the designated FV lock button (if utilized) once again to release the flash exposure if your next photo will have a different composition.
14. **Exposure confirmed**. The flash won't always need to be fully charged. If the flash indicator in the viewfinder blinks for around three seconds after the exposure, the whole flash charge was used, which may not have been sufficient for an appropriate exposure? Check that your image is not underexposed by seeing it on the display, and if it is, modify the settings (such as boosting the ISO on the Z8) to rectify the issue.

Flash Exposure Compensation

If your flash does not provide enough exposure, you can manually modify the Z8's computed flash exposure. You may link a button, such as Fn1, to Flash Mode/Flash Compensation using the Photo Shooting Menu's Flash Compensation option or Custom Setting f2: Custom Control Assignment. Once a button has been assigned, you may change Flash Compensation by pressing and holding it while spinning the sub-command dial, or Flash Mode by depressing it while using the main command dial. Adjustments between -3 EV and +1 EV can be done in 1/3 EV increments. As with standard exposure compensation, the adjustment you make is only effective until you hit the Flash button and move the sub-command dial until "0" appears on the monochrome control panel and in the viewfinder. To see the current flash exposure compensation setting, press the Flash button. While utilizing compensation, a symbol appears in the viewfinder and on the control panel. You may use Custom Setting e3:

Exposure Compensation for Flash to balance ambient light and flash exposure over the whole frame, or you can focus just on the backdrop. When exposure compensation is used, the camera adjusts the flash level. (The Z8 has distinct settings for ambient light adaption and flash exposure adjustment.) When employing flash, you may adjust either individually or simultaneously. This parameter only affects ambient exposure compensation when flash is used in conjunction with exposure compensation. **The fact that a portion of the light comes from a flash unit determines how ambient exposure correction is handled.**

- **Whole frame**. When you apply ambient exposure compensation (click the EV button on top of the camera to the right of the ISO button and turn the main command dial), both ambient and flash exposure compensation are adjusted throughout the whole frame. As a consequence, the exposure for the two components is balanced.

- **Just background**. When this option is selected, only the ambient exposure compensation is adjusted; the flash exposure compensation remains unaffected. Only the areas of your image in the background—which are often lighted by ambient light—get exposure correction as a consequence. The flash exposure correction is unaffected.

Specifying Flash Shutter Speed

This is an additional method for controlling the shutter speed that the Z8 will use while using flash. In contrast to Custom Setting e1: Flash Sync Speed, this parameter shows the slowest shutter speed that is possible for electronic flash synchronization while not in "slow sync" mode. When aiming to avoid ghost images caused by secondary exposure, use the maximum shutter speed compatible with your flash. This option prohibits both ambient light and the flash from being caught by the shutter speed chosen by the aperture-priority or programmable modes, which both choose the shutter speed for you. If you don't specifically choose slow sync, slow rear-curtain sync, or red-eye reduction with slow sync, the Z8 will avoid utilizing shutter speeds slower than the one you set with electronic flash. This amount might be between 30 and 1/60 of a second. If you believe you can keep the Z8 steady, a value of 1/30 s is a decent compromise; if your hands are shaking, use 1/60 s or greater. If you have tight grips or a lens that decreases vibration, use the 1/15 s option. However, keep in mind that Custom option e1 controls the default shutter speed; this option just influences the slowest shutter speed that will be utilized.

Previewing Your Flash Effect

The Nikon Z8's compatible external units, such as the SB-5000, SB-910, SB-700, and certain previous versions, may imitate a modeling light in the form of a series of repeated light flashes, allowing you to predict the influence the strobe will have when used for the main exposure. Even though this modeling flash, which can be switched on or off using Custom Setting e5, is not a perfect alternative for a genuine incandescent or fluorescent modeling light, it may help you understand how your subject will be lit and identify any possible shadow issues. When this feature is enabled, pushing the control momentarily initiates the modeling flash for your preview if you have set the Preview (depth-of-field) behavior to a custom button. The functionality may be turned off by choosing Off. The depth-of-field preview button should usually be left on if you don't want the modeling flash to fire when the flash unit is charged and ready unless you want to use it for depth-of-field (imagine that). External flash devices with modeling flash buttons are the SB-5000 and SB-910.

Flash Control

The Nikon SB-5000, SB-500, SB-400, and SB-300 Speedlights are more recent electronic flash units that may be modified using the Flash Control option in the Photo Shooting Menu. Any other Nikon electronic flash units, such as the SB-600, SB-700, SB-800, SB-900, and SB-910, must be adjusted using the flash's settings. Not all of the Speedlights mentioned below can reach them. For example, the SB-400 only supports manual exposure and TTL output modes. Unavailable choices will be greyed out. To utilize the Flash Control menu option, the flash must be placed on the Z8's hot shoe, turned on, and not in Remote mode. Depending on the characteristics of the flash unit you are using, the precise settings available from the Flash Control menu will vary. The graphic below depicts some or all of the options available on the first screen.

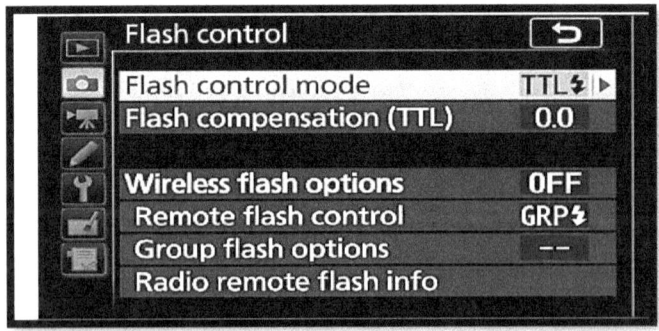

The image below displays the SB-5000's Flash Control Mode screen.

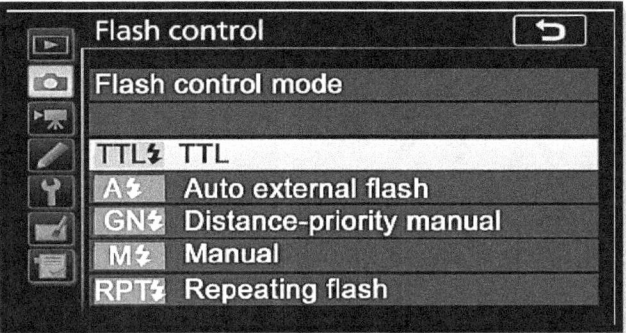

Working with Nikon Flash External Units

Nikon provides a wide range of CLS-compatible external flash units, from the flagship SB-5000 to the entry-level SB-300. Nikon may also produce other Speedlights soon. In addition, previous versions such as the SB-600, SB-400, SB-800, and SB-910/SB-900, which were either formally or informally discontinued, are still available in both new and used condition. The SB-600, SB-400, SB-800, and SB-910/SB-900 are among the previous variants.

Nikon SB-300

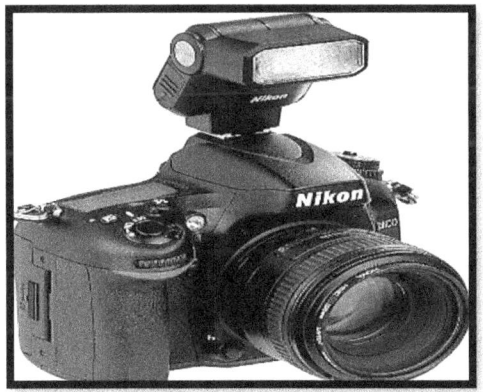

The Nikon SB-300 is a small external flash unit intended to improve the lighting capabilities of Nikon cameras. The SB-300, part of Nikon's Speedlight range, is an entry-level flash with a simple and user-friendly interface, making it suitable for novices and hobbyists wishing to get into creative lighting. The Nikon SB-300 has a sleek and lightweight design, making it a compact accessory that can be conveniently stored in your camera bag. It has a tilting flash head, which allows you to bounce the light off ceilings or walls for more natural and appealing illumination. The construction quality is strong, assuring longevity even after extended usage. It is compatible with Nikon digital SLR cameras that have a hot shoe. Before purchasing the flash, make sure that it is compatible with your camera model. As an entry-level flash, the SB-300 is frequently suggested for Nikon users looking to upgrade from the built-in camera flash and explore more creative lighting possibilities. The Nikon SB-300 has two basic flash modes: Manual and i-TTL. In i-TTL mode, the flash detects available light via the camera's lens and automatically adjusts the flash output to ensure balanced exposure. This is especially handy for photographers who are new to external flash units and want a more direct approach to lighting. In Manual mode, you have complete control over the flash output, which allows for greater creative freedom. Adjusting the flash power manually allows you to experiment with different lighting ratios and create unique lighting effects. It's crucial to remember that the SB-300 isn't as powerful as other of Nikon's more expensive Speedlights. It has a reference number of around 18 meters at ISO 100, making it more suited for close-up or portrait photography than long-distance or outdoor applications. One of the Nikon SB-300's important features is the ability to tilt the flash head, which allows you to bounce light off neighboring things like ceilings or walls. Bounce flash helps to disperse light and create softer shadows, producing more natural-looking photographs with less harshness. Although the SB-300 lacks built-in light modifiers like more modern Speedlights, you may use external light modifiers like diffusers and bounce cards to better control and shape the light. These modifiers may be added to the flash head to create various lighting effects and improve the overall quality of your photographs. Unlike several higher-end Nikon Speedlights, the SB-300 lacks built-in wireless capability for off-camera flash configurations. It may, however, be used as a remote flash when linked with a master flash that is compatible with Nikon's Creative Lighting System.

To utilize the SB-300 off-camera, you must remotely trigger it using another suitable Nikon flash as the master unit. This configuration enables more creative lighting combinations, such as employing the SB-300 as a fill light and the on-camera flash as the primary light source. The SB-300's tiny size and lightweight construction make it very portable, making it an ideal tool for photographers who are always on the move. Whether you're traveling, attending events, or shooting in a variety of settings, the SB-300 won't weigh you down or take up much room in your camera bag. While the Nikon SB-300 is a superb entry-level flash, it does have certain restrictions that should be noted before purchasing. Its power output may not be adequate for some photography settings, including outdoor events or large group photographs. Furthermore, the SB-300 lacks wireless capabilities, so you'll need to invest in extra equipment (such as a suitable master flash) if you want to explore more intricate off-camera lighting setups.

Nikon SB-400

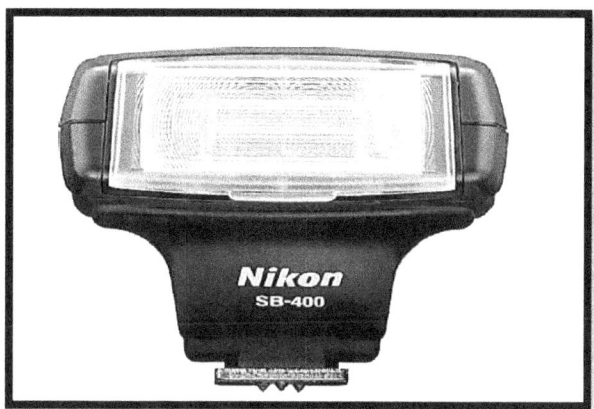

The Nikon SB-400 is a tiny, lightweight, and adaptable Speedlight flash unit built specifically for Nikon DSLR cameras. Nikon introduced the SB-400 in 2006, and it soon became popular among novice and enthusiast photographers because of its simplicity, ease of use, and great performance in varied lighting settings. The Nikon SB-400 has a sleek, simple style that complements Nikon DSLR cameras wonderfully. It measures around 66mm x 56mm x 80mm and weighs around 127 grams without batteries. Its small size makes it easy to transport in a camera bag or pocket, making it a popular choice among on-the-go photographers. The flash head may be angled upwards up to 90 degrees, allowing for bounce flash, which aids in achieving more natural and appealing lighting by reflecting light off ceilings or walls. The design incorporates a built-in diffuser to further soften the light output, making it excellent for portrait photography and inside shooting. Given its plastic structure, the build quality is typically strong, although it may not endure rigorous handling or inclement weather as well as other higher-end versions. However, most customers find the build quality adequate for daily usage. The Nikon SB-400 is intended to be user-friendly, and its controls reflect that idea. It features a power switch and two major buttons: "Mode" and "Zoom." The "Mode" button allows you to choose between automated and manual settings. In automated mode, the flash unit connects with the camera's metering system and adjusts its output, making it ideal for casual photos.

The "Zoom" button lets you manually change the flash coverage angle to fit the focal length of your lens. It has an angle range of 18mm to 135mm, making it suitable for a variety of lenses and shooting situations. The SB-400 lacks wireless connectivity and sophisticated capabilities featured in more costly Nikon Speedlights, like High-Speed Sync (HSS), Master/Remote control, and Multi-flash modes. While this may be a disadvantage for experienced photographers who need these complex functions, it makes the SB-400 basic and straightforward to use for beginners and amateurs. In terms of performance, the Nikon SB-400 delivers a high flash output given its size. The guiding number of 21m at ISO 100 is adequate for most indoor and close-range photography. The flash recycles fast, enabling rapid-fire shooting without long wait times between flashes. The automated mode performs an excellent job of measuring and generating a balanced fill flash, especially when the ambient illumination is insufficient. It greatly enhances image quality in circumstances including strong shadows or backlit subjects. One of the SB-400's key features is its bounce flash capabilities. It allows you to bounce the flash against a ceiling or wall, creating softer, more natural-looking light that is ideal for portraiture. This function increases the flash's adaptability and provides a significant advantage over built-in camera flashes, which lack such flexibility. The Nikon SB-400 is a great entry-level flash, but it has certain restrictions. Its power output may not be adequate for some professional applications or outdoor photography, particularly in intense sunshine. Photographers shooting under similar conditions may prefer a more powerful Speedlight with extra functions. Because of its lack of wireless capabilities, the SB-400 cannot be utilized as a remote flash or in a multi-flash system. This is a severe drawback for photographers who demand intricate lighting configurations and creative lighting management. Furthermore, the SB-400 lacks a built-in swivel head, limiting its capacity to bounce light off walls from various angles. It simply tilts up, limiting the variety of the bounce flash approach.

Nikon SB-500

At ISO 100, this Nikon flash unit costs $250 and has a guide number of 24/79. It also has a fast recycle time of about 3.5 seconds and can operate for up to 140 flashes on two AA batteries. It has a built-in LED video light with three unique output levels that may also be utilized as fill light for still photography, especially when turned up to its maximum setting. In wireless mode, it functions well, providing access to four wireless channels as well as two groups via its Commander mode. The SB-500's head can be tilted up to 90 degrees, with click stops at 0, 60, 75, and 90. It spins horizontally 180 degrees to the left and right, providing a variety of illumination options via a bounce flash. If you need a zoom head to modify the flash output to evenly spread light at different focal lengths, the SB-700 is the way to go; however, it has a restricted zoom range because it cannot zoom in or out. In the image below, the SB-500 is connected to a Nikon Z8 via the SC-28 cable and hooked to the Nikon SK-7 bracket (available separately) as shown. In its current state, this structure has a few advantages. Second, when the flash is positioned to the side, it moves further away from the lens's axis, offering further red-eye protection. You may get bounce effects by tilting the flash. Because there's no top-heavy flash unit above the camera, I find this configuration much simpler to handle and less ungainly.

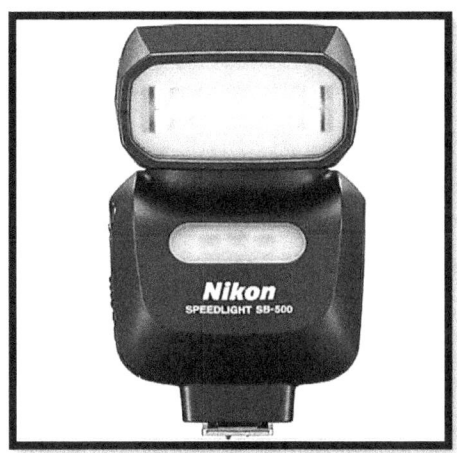

The nicest part is that you can quickly unhook the flash or the SC-28 from the bracket and utilize them separately from the camera. The Flash believes it is still directly connected to the Z8, and it is. There is no need to experiment with wifi modes, channels, groups, or other settings since there are none. The model number SC-29 refers to an auxiliary cable that is nine feet long and has built-in focus aid lights. I own both, but I prefer to mount the SC-29's focus-assist light on top of the Z8 camera. If the Z8 needs a bit more light to focus well, the lamp may be directed in this fashion. Although the SB-500 includes a focus light, there is no guarantee that it will concentrate on your subject when you need it.

Nikon SB-700

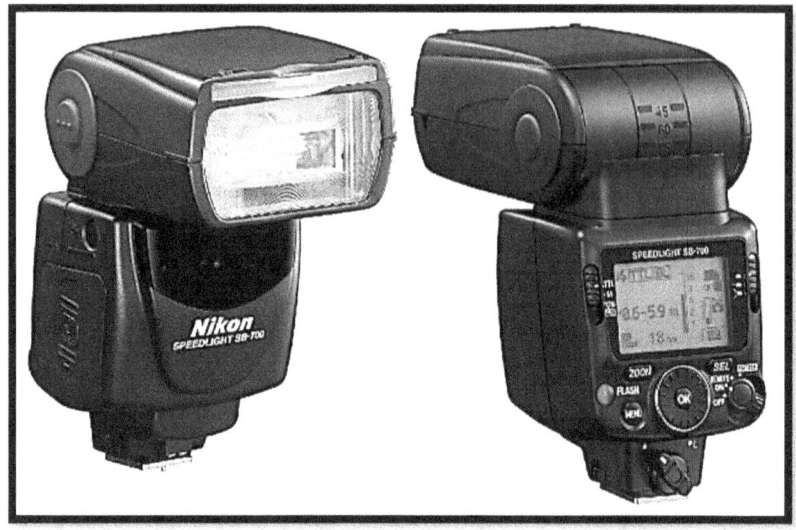

The Nikon SB-700 is a versatile and powerful Speedlight flash unit designed for Nikon DSLR cameras. It was introduced by Nikon in 2010 as a successor to the popular SB-600 flash. The SB-700 is aimed at both enthusiasts and professional photographers, offering a wide range of features and capabilities to enhance the quality of lighting in various shooting scenarios.

Design and Build Quality

The Nikon SB-700 has a well-designed, small, and strong body that complements Nikon DSLR cameras. Its dimensions are around 71.0mm x 126.0mm x 104.5mm, and it weighs around 360 grams without batteries, achieving an excellent blend of mobility and strength. The SB-700's flash head can be tilted and rotated, allowing for better control over the flash's output. It can tilt up to 90 degrees for bounce flash and spin 180 degrees left and right, allowing you to bounce the flash off walls or other objects at a variety of angles. The SB-700's user interface is clear and intuitive. It has a big, easy-to-read LCD screen, separate buttons for each setting, and a navigation dial for rapid adjustments. The buttons are well-placed, and the menu system is properly arranged, making it easy to access and configure numerous flash settings.

Features and Controls

The Nikon SB-700 has a wide range of functions that will meet the demands of both beginner and professional photographers. It offers three alternative lighting patterns: Standard, Center-weighted, and Even, allowing for greater versatility in light distribution for diverse objects and settings. One of the SB-700's distinguishing qualities is its ability to operate as a Master or Remote flash unit in Nikon's Creative Lighting System (CLS). As a Master unit, it can wirelessly control additional Nikon Speedlights, allowing for unique multi-flash configurations. As a Remote unit, it may be controlled by another Master unit, making complicated lighting configurations simple. The flash zoom range extends from 24mm to 120mm and may be changed automatically or manually to fit the focal length of the lens. The SB-700 also features a High-Speed Sync (HSS), which allows users to employ flash at high shutter speeds to freeze moving subjects even in harsh ambient light. It also contains a built-in diffuser and bounce card, which further increases its adaptability by softening the light output and providing fill light when bouncing is not possible.

Performance

The Nikon SB-700 performs admirably in terms of flash power; recycle speed, and general dependability. With a guide number of 28m at ISO 100, it provides a significant increase in flash output over entry-level Speedlights such as the SB-400. This makes it suited for a variety of lighting settings, such as outdoor shots and bigger indoor venues. The SB-700's short recycle time allows photographers to fire off consecutive flashes without significant delay. It aids in the capturing of fast-paced activity and assures consistent outcomes in circumstances requiring precise timing. The SB-700 has exceptional flash exposure precision because of its i-TTL (intelligent Through-The-Lens) flash control. The i-TTL technology interacts with the camera's metering and focusing algorithms to provide exact flash exposure dependent on the subject's distance and ambient light conditions.

Limitations

The Nikon SB-700 is a strong and flexible Speedlight, however it may not meet the demands of professional photographers who want more sophisticated capabilities and higher power output. In challenging settings, such as sports or wildlife photography, a higher powerful flash unit, such as the Nikon SB-5000, may be preferable. Another disadvantage for photographers who regularly shoot in harsh outside circumstances is a lack of weatherproofing. While the SB-700 is quite strong, it may not be as lasting as higher-end speed lights with weather-resistant construction.

Nikon SB-R200

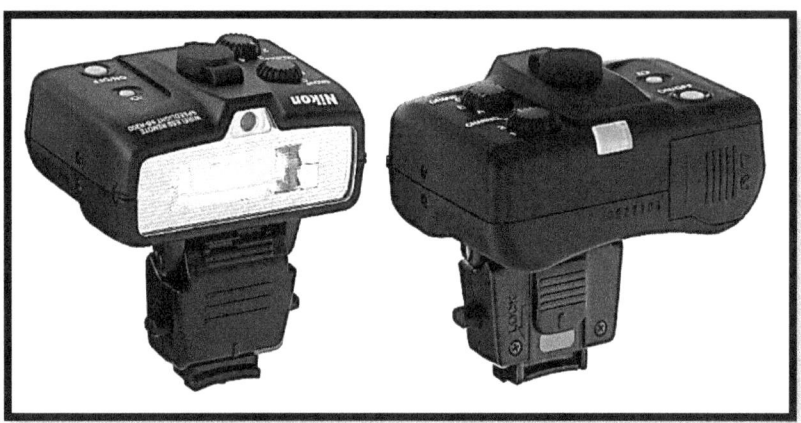

The Nikon SB-R200 is a wireless speedlight that is both tiny and adaptable. It is designed to work with Nikon's Creative Lighting System. It was first available in 2005 as part of the Nikon R1C1 Wireless Close-Up Speedlight System, a package aimed at close-up and macro photography aficionados. The SB-R200 has a variety of features and functions that make it an outstanding choice for close-up photography. It may also be used as a remote flash unit in conjunction with other Nikon speedlights.

Key Features and Specifications

Compact and Lightweight:
- **Description**: The Nikon SB-R200 is a small, lightweight flash unit that can be easily mounted on the front of a lens using the included SX-1 Attachment Ring or on various Nikon Speedlight mounts.
- **Benefit**: Its portability and ease of use make it suitable for on-the-go photographers.

Wireless Connectivity:
- **Description**: The SB-R200 is a wireless speedlight that can be triggered remotely using Nikon's Advanced Wireless Lighting (AWL) system.
- **Benefit**: It can be controlled and triggered from a compatible master flash, such as the Nikon SB-800, SB-900, or the commander built into compatible Nikon DSLR cameras, allowing for versatile and creative lighting setups.

Flexible Lighting Control:
- **Description**: Offers a range of lighting options including TTL (Through-The-Lens) mode, Manual mode, and Remote mode.
- **Benefit**: In TTL mode, the flash output is automatically adjusted for proper exposure. Manual mode allows precise control over the lighting, and Remote mode enables wireless control as part of a multiple-flash setup.

LED Modeling Light:
- **Description**: Equipped with a continuous LED modeling light to preview lighting and shadow effects before capturing the shot.
- **Benefit**: This feature is particularly useful in macro photography, providing precise control over lighting.

Fast Recycling Time:
- **Description**: The flash unit boasts a quick recycling time.
- **Benefit**: Allows for rapid shooting without significant delays between shots, ensuring you don't miss critical moments.

Flash Head Positioning:
- **Description**: The SB-R200's flash head can be tilted up to 60 degrees and rotated up to 120 degrees.
- **Benefit**: Provides greater flexibility in directing the light, enhancing creative control over lighting angles and effects.

Close-Up Accessories:
- **Description**: Typically sold as part of the Nikon R1C1 Wireless Close-Up Speedlight System, which includes accessories like the SX-1 Attachment Ring and the optional SW-11 Extreme Close-Up Positioning Adapter.
- **Benefit**: These accessories enable precise control in macro photography, making it easier to achieve detailed and well-lit close-up shots.

Compatibility:
- **Description**: Compatible with Nikon's i-TTL flash control system and works with a wide range of Nikon DSLR cameras that support the CLS system.
- **Benefit**: It is an excellent complement to other Nikon speedlights for multi-flash setups, enhancing the overall versatility and functionality of your lighting equipment.

Nikon SB-910

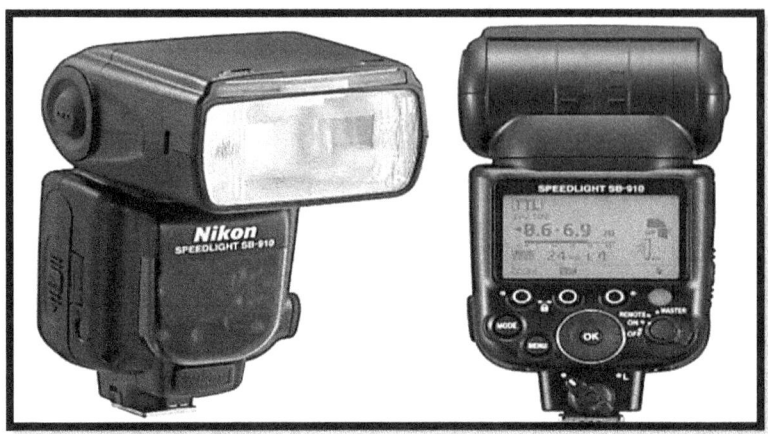

In the time leading up to the launch of the SB-5000 model, the Nikon SB-910 was widely regarded as the company's most technologically advanced flash unit. Despite this, Nikon's SB-910 flash unit continues to be one of the company's most popular offerings (together with the SB-900, which was its predecessor). When the "zooming" flash head is set to the 35mm position, the guide number is 34/111.5 (meters/foot), and it is still available new or secondhand for around $400. This is because it allows you to adjust the lens's coverage angle. It also includes some extra features including a Commander mode, a repeating flash, a modeling light, and customizable power output. The SB-910 is a mild reboot of the earlier SB-900, which had a bad reputation for overheating and shutting down after a few consecutive exposures. As a result, the SB-900 was replaced with the SB-910, which is essentially a minor reboot of the original SB-900. The SB-900 could only take a limited number of shots in a sequence before shutting down automatically (approximately a dozen), making it perfect for scenarios when you need to capture multiple photos rapidly. Despite having its thermal protection mechanism, the SB-910 has the potential to overheat. The SB-910 does not turn off the flash as the unit warms up; instead, it increases the amount of time between each flash, giving the gadget more time to cool down before the next shot is captured. When the SB-910 recognizes that the device is beginning to warm up, it does not switch off the flash.

Instead, it increases the amount of time between each flash. This "upgrade" is not a true remedy, but it does encourage you to slow down your shooting pace somewhat to get a few more flashes out of this Speedlight before it needs to be turned off for further cooling. If you do this, you should be able to obtain a few extra flashes from this Speedlight. Nikon predicts that if you use AA batteries with a capacity of 2600 mAh and rechargeable batteries (which gradually become longer as the flash heats up and thermal protection kicks in), you should be able to get 190 flashes out of the SB-910 if you fire the Speedlight at its maximum output once every 30 seconds and have a minimum recycle time of 2.3 seconds. This assumes a minimum recycling time of 2.3 seconds. According to Nikon's calculations, turning off the AF-assist lights, power zoom, and LCD panel illumination allows for the most photos to be taken with a single set of batteries. This is because all of these things consume large amounts of electricity. Although there have been some improvements, like illuminated buttons and a restyled soft cover, the SB-910 is fundamentally comparable to the SB-900, which we Nikon photographers have come to know and dread. Despite these improvements, the SB-910 is essentially the same product. However, there have been substantial advancements. For example, you may produce a bounce flash by tilting and whirling the light in the opposite direction of the subject. It can "zoom" and extend out its coverage angle to illuminate the field of vision of lenses with focal lengths ranging from 8mm to 200mm, and it has extra exposure settings not provided by the lens itself. The light sensor incorporated in the equipment is responsible for making these functions available to the user.

Even when it is attached to the Z8 and not being used off-camera, the unit is placed higher, which helps to reduce reflections from the eye back onto the camera lens. This holds even when the device is not utilized off-camera. As a result, red-eye symptoms are alleviated. Furthermore, both the SB-910 and SB-900 include their own highly effective focus assist lamp, which allows for autofocus even in low-light circumstances. My SB-910 is powered by Panasonic (formerly Sanyo) Eneloop AA nickel metal hydride batteries. These batteries were manufactured by Eneloop. They are a sort of rechargeable battery that is pre-equipped with a characteristic that allows them to perform properly when used in electrical flashes, which sets them apart from other batteries. Unlike ordinary batteries, Eneloop cells do not self-discharge after a set length of time. They may keep their juice for at least a year after they are charged. As a consequence, you don't have to worry about the batteries running out of juice in between usage; instead, keep a couple in your Speedlight and a few backups in your camera bag. One of the most frustrating things that may happen is turning on your strobe after not using it in a month only to realize that the batteries have expired. This is one of the scenarios in which this may occur. You should be aware that the SB-910's firmware, like your camera's firmware, may be upgraded. If you look at the readouts for the customized settings on the flash, you may determine which firmware version you are presently using. If an update is necessary, you will need to visit Nikon's website to acquire the updated firmware module. After putting it into a memory card, you should install the flash on your Z8 and power it on. After that, turn on the power. A fourth option will appear in the "Firmware" portion of the Setup menu, represented by a "S." (which stands for speedlight or strobe). The SB-910's firmware can be updated in the same way as the camera's firmware can be updated via the connection between the camera and the flash.

SB-5000

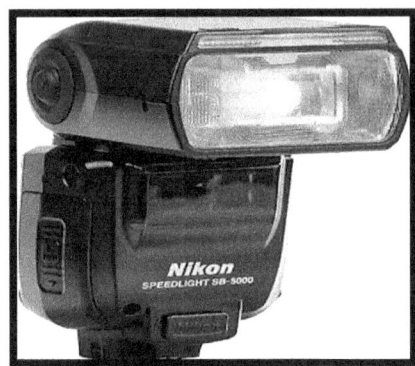

The Nikon SB-5000 is a powerful and versatile wireless speedlight flash unit designed for professional photographers and advanced enthusiasts. Released as part of Nikon's Creative Lighting System (CLS), the SB-5000 offers a wide range of features and capabilities that make it a top choice for photographers seeking high-performance lighting solutions for various shooting scenarios.

Key Features and Specifications

Radio Control Wireless Flash:
- **Description**: Built-in radio control system allowing wireless communication between the flash and compatible Nikon cameras.
- **Benefit**: Provides greater reliability and range compared to traditional optical wireless systems, even in bright outdoor environments or when the flash is not within direct line of sight.

Advanced Wireless Lighting (AWL):
- **Description**: Functions as a master flash, controlling and triggering multiple remote flashes in up to six groups.
- **Benefit**: Enables sophisticated lighting setups, making it ideal for portrait, studio, and event photographers who require precise control over their lighting arrangements.

Powerful Output and High-Speed Performance:

- **Description**: Guide number of approximately 34 meters at ISO 100 and a focal length of 35mm, with fast recycling time.
- **Benefit**: Ensures ample illumination for various shooting conditions and allows for rapid continuous shooting without significant delays.

Cool Down Function:
- **Description**: Automatically reduces flash output if the flash head detects overheating.
- **Benefit**: Prevents overheating during intensive use, maintaining consistent performance and protecting the flash from potential damage.

Support for Radio-Controlled and Optical-Controlled Groups:
- **Description**: Backward compatible with Nikon's optical CLS system.
- **Benefit**: Can be used as a remote flash with older Nikon cameras and other Nikon speedlights that support the optical wireless system.

Quick and Intuitive Controls:
- **Description**: Easy-to-navigate LCD screen and intuitive controls, supporting a unified flash control menu on compatible Nikon cameras.
- **Benefit**: Streamlines the setup process, offering a seamless user experience and allowing photographers to make adjustments quickly and efficiently.

Customizable Functions:
- **Description**: Range of customizable functions to tailor the flash's behavior to specific shooting preferences.
- **Benefit**: Adapts to different shooting scenarios and creative needs, providing a high level of personalization.

Compatibility:
- **Description**: Compatible with a wide range of Nikon DSLR cameras that support the CLS system, including Nikon's high-end professional models.
- **Benefit**: Can be used in combination with older Nikon speed lights that are compatible with the optical CLS system, enhancing versatility and functionality.

Using Zoom Heads

When referring to some flash units, notably speedlights, and studio strobes, the term "zoom heads" refers to a particular functional component. In this particular setting, the term "zoom" does not refer to the digital communication platform Zoom; rather, it refers to the aspect of the flash head that allows for the focal length to be adjusted. For the sake of enhancing lighting control in photography, let's investigate what zoom heads are and how they work. Changing the coverage angle of the flash's output may be accomplished by the use of zoom heads, which are flash heads that can be mechanically changed. The major objective of the zoom function is to ensure that the flash coverage is optimized to correspond with the focal length of the lens that is being utilized. When utilizing multiple lens focal lengths, guarantees that the light from the flash is focused on the subject, significantly reducing the amount of light that spills over and giving lighting that is both more efficient and more even. The focal length of a lens is always measured in millimeters, and the zoom range of a flash head is often measured in millimeters as well. For instance, a flash may have a zoom range of 24-105mm, which indicates that it can alter the flash beam to cover angles ranging from a broad 24mm to a more concentrated 105mm.

Here's how heads work zoom and how they can be beneficial in various photography scenarios:

- **Matching the Focal Length**: The angle of view shifts whenever you use a zoom lens that has a focal length that is different from the one you are using. The zoom head can modify its coverage so that it corresponds with the lens's field of view. This ensures that the light from the flash lands on the subject in the correct manner and does not spread out too much. This prevents the light from being wasted and reduces the likelihood of overexposure occurring in certain areas of the image.

- **Preventing Vignetting**: If you take wide-angle photographs without changing the flash coverage, you run the risk of experiencing vignetting, which is a reduction in the brightness of the corners of the frame. It is possible to eliminate or reduce the amount of vignetting by moving the zoom head to a wider angle. This will allow the light to be distributed more evenly.

- **Controlling Light Spill**: When you require exact control over the direction of light, employing a zoom head will help you focus the light on the subject and limit light spills on the backdrop or other regions that are not intended to be lighted. This is especially helpful in circumstances when you need to manage accurate light direction.

- **Enhancing Efficiency**: You can guarantee that the power of the flash is utilized more efficiently by adjusting the coverage of the flash to match the focal length of the lens. This allows you to use lower flash power settings for a particular photo, which can conserve the battery life of the camera and minimize the amount of time that passes between flashes.

- **Versatility in Lighting Setups**: The flash is more adaptable in a variety of photography circumstances because it can modify the magnification of the flash head. Whether you are photographing close-ups, landscapes, or portraits, the Zoom head can quickly adjust to meet the precise requirements of each circumstance.

It's essential to note that not all flash units have zoom heads. The feature is more commonly found in advanced speedlights and high-end studio strobes. When choosing a flash unit, especially if you need the zoom feature, be sure to check the specifications and capabilities of the specific model you are considering.

Flash Modes

Nine distinct categories may be applied to digital single-lens reflex cameras, ranging from the most contemporary digital single-lens reflex cameras to certain historical digital single-lens reflex cameras and even earlier video cameras. External flash units come with a variety of flash modes that are built in. Some of these flash modes are compatible with specific types of cameras, while others are not compatible with those sorts of cameras. The bulk of the groups are shown in a table inside the instructions for external flash devices; however, users of the Z8 do not have any need to be concerned about this table in any manner (unless, of course, you also have an older digital or video SLR). The Nikon D1-series cameras and the Nikon D100 are examples of digital cameras that do not comply with the Nikon Creative Lighting System (CLS). Digital cameras may be roughly classified into two groups: those that are compatible with the CLS and those that are not. The latter type is the one that the Z8 belongs to. There is a vast range of video SLRs available, and they are classified I through VII according to the feature combinations that they can manage as a whole. It is not necessary to pay attention to such settings unless you are concurrently utilizing an old video camera and an external flash.

However, before you can spin the multi-selector to select the required mode, you must first push the right button on the rotary multi-selector. This will bring the flash mode on the SB-5000 to the forefront of your attention. The confirmation button is positioned in the middle of the screen. Press the MODE button, which is located on the left side of the rear of the SB-910 or SB-900, and then let go of it while spinning the selection dial until the mode that you want displays on the LCD. Immediately after that, a detailed explanation of the several TTL automatic flash modes will be provided. (The SB-700 Speedlight has a sliding mode selection button that may be found to the left of the LCD. This switches offers GN, TTL, and Manual modes of operation as possible options. When the flash is operating in Master mode, the control panel will only display those two modes from the available options. **On the other hand, the SB-700 is capable of functioning in repeating mode when it is utilized as a remote flash that is activated by a Master Commander flash.**

- **iTTL Automatic Balanced Fill Flash**. The flash and the camera's Matrix and Center-weighted exposure modes combine to create an exposure balance that guarantees that both the main subject and the background are adequately lit. A TTL BL indicator is seen on the LCD. However, the flash will return to the standard iTTL setting if you alter the metering mode to Spot.

- **Standard iTTL**. The exposure for the primary subject is determined by this mode, which is activated when the Spot metering mode is selected (or if you have fixed the flash exposure using FV Lock). The exposure for the backdrop is not taken into consideration in this mode. There is just one exposure that is measured and taken into consideration for the computation, and that is the exposure of the flash. An indication of the TTL is displayed on the LCD. If you use the flash at its maximum power when the camera is operating in either the iTTL Automatic Balanced Fill-Flash mode or the Standard iTTL mode, the ready-light indication will flash for three seconds both on the flash itself and in the viewfinder of the camera. Even if you had used the flash at its highest level, it would not have been sufficient to achieve the desired exposure. This is something that you should take into consideration as a warning. Under these circumstances, the LCD will flash a ready-light sign as well as an EV indication, displaying the level of underexposure as -0.3 to -3.0 EV.

- **AA: Auto Aperture flash**. If you choose to use this mode, the LCD will display an indication that contains the letter "A" and a symbol that represents an aperture or lens opening simultaneously. The amount of flash illumination that is reflected from the subject is measured by a built-in light sensor in either the SB-5000 or the SB-910/SB-900. The output is adjusted to create the appropriate exposure based on the ISO, aperture, focal length, and flash compensation values that are set on the Z8. This makes it possible to achieve the desired exposure. By utilizing this option on the flash, you can control the exposure by using either the Program or Aperture-Priority modes to control the exposure. This mode, along with the A and GN modes, are holdovers from earlier generations of Nikon cameras. This option was included to ensure compatibility with the Panasonic Z8. It is not relevant to the Z8 in any way.

- **A: Non-TTL auto flash**. When utilized in this mode, the sensor of the Speedlight monitors the flashlight that is reflected off of the subject being photographed. Following that, the output is modified such that it provides the appropriate exposure. Additionally, in contrast to the AA mode, this option does not make use of any input on the aperture setting of the camera. It is possible to utilize this setting on the flash when the Z8 is set to either the Manual shooting mode or the Aperture-priority shooting mode. Because increasing the aperture setting of the lens will result in either more or less exposure, you may utilize this option to manually "bracket" shots instead of using the aperture setting. Since the flash is not aware of the aperture value of the lens, it is impossible to discern the aperture that you have changed to.

GN: Distance priority manual. Whether you are using the Aperture-priority or Manual exposure modes, the SB-5000 or SB-910/SB 900 will automatically change the light output in accordance with the distance, ISO, and aperture to get the required exposure. By navigating to the Flash Control menu when using the SB-5000, you will be able to access this particular option. By pushing the MODE button on the SB-910/SB-900 flash and twisting the selection dial until the GN indication appears, the GN indicator may be enabled. It is important to note that the GN option is only displayed when the flash is pointed in a forward direction or when it is in the downward bounce position. After that, you will need to hit the OK button to confirm your option. After hitting the Function 2 button, you will then be able to pick a shooting distance by turning the selection dial until the proper shooting distance is displayed on the LCD. This will allow you to achieve the desired shooting distance. If you would like to confirm your option, please click the OK button. If the exposure mode is set to Manual, the SB-5000 or SB-910/SB-900 will suggest an aperture for you to choose from on the lens that is linked to the Z8.

M: Manual flash. The flash's output remains unchanged throughout the entirety of its duration. While you continue to hold down the MODE button, turn the selection dial until the letter M appears on the LCD screen. All that is required of you is to click the OK button to validate your choices. With the SB-5000 and the majority of other Nikon Speedlights, you can select the desired power output level. The SB-5000 has the capability of reaching a power output level as low as 1/128th. You can decide the appropriate f-stop to use by taking a few trial photographs, making use of a flash meter, or simply going by the seat of your trousers. The next step is to select the f/stop that you want to use, and then change the exposure mode on the Z8 to either Aperture-priority or Manual.

RPT: Repeating flash. When the flash fires several times in rapid succession, it produces a multiple flash strobing effect. Make sure your Z8's exposure mode is set to Manual before using this mode. Then, modify the frequency, flash output power, and the number of successive flashes that take place in each frame.

Repeating Flash

Examples of external flashes with the ability to shoot repeated flashes include the SB-5000, SB-910, and SB-900. You can consult your handbook when using the handbook exposure mode to find out which buttons to press to make the following changes.

Follow these steps:

- **Flash should be in RPT mode**. With the SB-5000, choose repeated flash by first highlighting the mode by pushing the rotary multi-selector right button (the MODE button), and then choosing it by rotating the dial. The RPT symbol should display in the upper left corner of the LCD after pressing the MODE button on the SB-910/SB-900. Press the OK button to confirm.

- **Pick Flash Output Level**. You must select the flash power level you want to use while using these flash devices. This value indicates the range of possible flash counts based on the charge stored in the capacitor. To adjust the output level, use the SB-5000's flash mode buttons. Pressing the Function 2 or Function 1 button on the SB-910 or SB-900 will toggle the selection dial once the number of flashes is highlighted on the LCD (immediately to the right of the RPT signal). This may be accomplished with either the SB-910 or the SB-900. Any power level between 1/8 to 1/128 can be selected.
- **Select number of shots**. Choosing the total number of photographs that will make up your series is the next stage. Make use of the SB-5000's Times setting so you can choose the appropriate amount of flashes. With the SB-900, you will need to click the Function 2 button; with the SB-910, you can highlight the selection by hitting the Function 3 button. The maximum number of shots that may be chosen varies depending on the camera's shutter speed and firing frequency (described below).
- **Choose frequency: how many shots per second**. This determines how quickly the series is finished. Make sure the SB-5000 is set to the Hz setting. With the SB-900, you will need to click the Function 2 button; with the SB-910, you can highlight the selection by hitting the Function 3 button.

The maximum number of images that may be taken in a certain sequence is determined by the parameters of shutter speed, output level, and frequency that the photographer chooses to use. When the shutter speed is increased, the number of bursts that may be shot off at a particular frequency is restricted. This is because the many flashes can only be released when the shutter is entirely open. Both the high output levels and the high-frequency settings have the effect of rapidly depleting the capacitor with their respective effects. Therefore, the maximum number of bursts that are feasible will be determined by the combination that you select. Approximately ninety rounds are the maximum number of shots that may be expected from the SB-910 or SB-5000 while operating at a power of 1/64 or 1/128. Additionally, the burst frequency can range anywhere from one to three times per second. Such a large number of dismissals are spread out across a considerable amount of time (at least thirty seconds), which is a huge amount of time. With the SB-5000 and SB-910, you may achieve incredibly brief bursts of fire, with a maximum of twenty to one hundred firings per second and twenty-four firings at one-twelfth of the power. Nevertheless, the total number of flashes will be far smaller than before. Even after all has been said and done, there is still a significant amount of room for forward progress. It would take you more than five seconds to acquire 24 bursts if you were to use the 100Hz option, but if you used the 20Hz setting, it would take you only a little bit more than a second.

CHAPTER EIGHTEEN

SETTING UP A BANK FOR PHOTOGRAPHY

This chapter explains how to use the shooting menu banks to configure your Z8 camera for sport photography, landscape photography, and night photography. Menu banks, in essence, allow you to configure the Nikon Z8's menu in up to four distinct ways. You can label these four menus (for example, landscape, wildlife, portrait, and macro) and easily move between them to change the state of the Z8 depending on what you're capturing.

Shooting Menu Banks

Many of your fundamental camera settings, including picture quality, ISO sensitivity, focus mode, and vibration reduction, are saved in the Nikon Z8's Photo Shooting Menu. It is easy to save a Shooting Menu bank. First, go through the full Photo Shooting Menu and set up everything for the bank. For example, if you were creating a "landscapes" Shooting Menu Bank, you might set the ISO sensitivity to 64, turn off Auto ISO, and activate long exposure noise reduction. After you've completed creating the menu, navigate to "Shooting Menu Bank," click on it, and save or rename the bank. Even while the Nikon Z8's menu banks may be renamed from their default "A, B, C, D" labels, I recommend keeping it simple. If you don't use the majority of the banks every day, it's easy to build four unique menu banks with small variations between them and then ultimately forget about the differences.

Settings up a Bank for Sport Photography

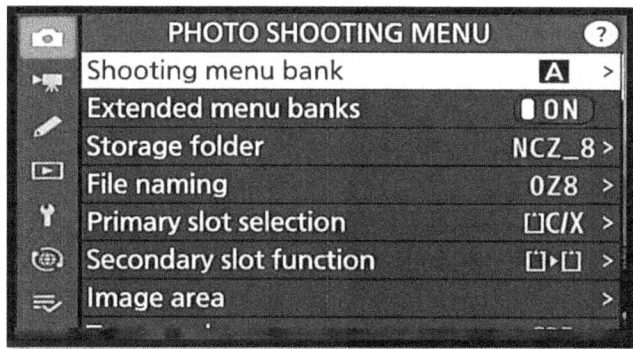

If you go to Menu and select the first item under the camera icon, "Shooting menu bank," you can choose your sports menu based on whatever alphabet you have allocated to it. When you enter the "Shooting menu bank," you can rename the options. When you select one of these options, everything you do to modify the menu is saved in that menu bank.

The settings for sports photography include:

Fast Continuous Shooting: 30.0fps

In the dynamic realm of sports photography, the adage "faster is superior" resonates profoundly. The Nikon Z8's rapid and continuous shooting rate of 30.0fps catapults it into a league where capturing swift actions is not merely a capability but an art form.

Environmental Safeguarding

Outdoor sports present a variety of climatic problems, necessitating the camera's ability to withstand harsh environments. This is a crucial necessity for weathering bad weather conditions such as rain and snow, as well as constant exposure to dust and water splashes.

Fast Max shutter speed: 1/32000s

A notable facet of the Nikon Z8 is its impressive maximum shutter speed of 1/32000s. This rapidity effectively immobilizes virtually all forms of sports action, simultaneously proving to be an asset when deploying fast lenses at their widest apertures under luminous sunlight.

493 Focus Points

In the context of sports photography, when the continuous autofocus (AFC) mode is frequently used to track subjects, the need for several focus points becomes clear. The Nikon Z8's massive assemblage of 493 focuses points results in increased precision and efficiency while tracking moving subjects.

Good Low Light ISO

In the realm of sports photography, where maintaining a swift shutter speed is imperative, the quality of high ISO performance cannot be understated. The Nikon Z8 excels in this facet, ensuring that a high ISO setting remains effective even in challenging low-light scenarios.

Wireless Connection

While wireless connectivity might not be universally utilized, professional sports photographers harness its capabilities for seamless file transfers. Eliminating the waiting period for memory card swapping, Wi-Fi connectivity enables swift and efficient transmission of files.

Good Ergonomics & Handling

The ergonomic design and proficient handling of the Nikon Z8's body solidify its stance as an ideal tool for sports photography. An array of external controls and well-conceived ergonomics contribute to effortless maneuverability during high-intensity sports shoots.

Electronic Built-in Viewfinder

During a frantic sports shot, the use of an electronic built-in viewfinder is a valuable advantage. This aspect not only develops stability by offering the photographer a stronger connection to the camera body but has also proven beneficial when presented with the obstacles given by bright sunshine making LCD panels difficult to understand.

Image Stabilization

The presence of image stabilization in the Nikon Z8 significantly mitigates the detriments of camera shake, particularly when dealing with extended focal lengths. This enhancement ensures the attainment of sharper, more visually captivating photographs within the demanding sphere of sports photography.

Anti-Flicker feature

Many sporting events are illuminated by flickering lights that can distort photographic outcomes. The incorporation of the anti-flicker feature within the Nikon Z8 counteracts this phenomenon, albeit with the trade-off of slightly reduced continuous shooting speed.

Setting up a Bank for Landscape Photography

Utilizing Live View

The utilization of Live View for meticulous focus adjustments surpasses the precision achievable through a traditional viewfinder. This modern approach grants a heightened level of accuracy when fine-tuning focus, enhancing the overall quality of the captured imagery.

Expansive Full-Frame Sensor Dimension (35.9 x 23.9 mm)

The Nikon Z8 features a big full-frame sensor with dimensions of 35.9 x 23.9 mm. This large sensor size ensures superb image quality in low-light conditions, well beyond the capabilities of smaller sensors. Furthermore, its bigger dimensions contribute to improved pixel quality, distinguishing it from sensors with lesser dimensions.

Remarkably High-Resolution Sensor: 46.0MP

Distinguishing itself as particularly adept for landscape photography, the Nikon Z8 boasts an impressive 46.0MP sensor. This substantial resolution capacity empowers the camera to meticulously capture intricate details within the landscape, subsequently facilitating the production of larger format prints that faithfully preserve these details.

Incorporated Environmental Sealing

Given that landscape photography is generally done in the unpredictable outdoors, the Nikon Z8 includes strong environmental sealing. This critical feature prepares the camera to face a wide range of weather situations, allowing the photographer to safely pursue their creative aspirations in a variety of meteorological scenarios. Making tiny focus changes with a live view is more exact than doing it with a viewfinder.

Setting up a Bank for Night Photography

Harness the Manual Exposure Mode of the Nikon Z8

Use your Nikon Z8's manual exposure mode for shooting in low-light conditions. Begin with ISO 1600 and an exposure time of 8-10 seconds. Combine this with the lens aperture completely open. Refine these values based on the features of your lens and the current conditions, altering as needed for best results.

Consistently Adopt a Fixed Daylight White Balance

For unwavering consistency in your nocturnal captures, adhere to a fixed daylight white balance setting on your Nikon Z8. This steadfast choice ensures that the color temperature remains unaltered across your images, fostering a harmonious visual narrative.

Disable Image Stabilization (VR/IS)

To uphold the precision of your night photography endeavors, deactivate the image stabilization (VR/IS) function on your Nikon Z8. By doing so, you prevent unintended corrections that might compromise the exactness of your long-exposure shots.

Tune Your Display Configuration

Enhance your nocturnal photography experience by meticulously configuring your display settings on the Nikon Z8. Dim the display brightness to its minimum setting and eliminate any superfluous shooting overlay data and grid lines. These adjustments culminate in a display that remains luminous without impinging upon your night vision acuity.

Opt for White Text on a Black LCD Background

Selecting a white text display over a black backdrop will improve the usefulness of your Nikon Z8 LCD in low-light conditions. This wise option permits simple navigation of settings and parameters without significantly interrupting your adaption to the prevailing ambient illumination.

Optimize Battery Longevity via Sleep and Display Timers

Configuring the camera's sleep and display timers to brief intervals, ideally less than 10 seconds, will extend the operating longevity of your Nikon Z8 battery. This prudent method conserves power without risking your ability to quickly re-engage in your photography pursuits.

Deactivate Non-Essential Wi-Fi Functions

Prioritize power efficiency by disabling any non-essential Wi-Fi functions that facilitate photo transmission while your Nikon Z8 is turned off. This judicious step minimizes energy consumption and ensures your camera remains primed for action when needed.

Favor Electronic Front-Curtain Shutter

Choose the electronic front-curtain shutter from the available shutter choices for your Nikon Z8. This decision reduces the likelihood of vibrations and artifacts, particularly when photographing sensitive nighttime and long-exposure compositions.

Attain Precise Focus before Nightfall

Ensure you have the best focus possible before total darkness falls. This is especially important when using autofocus lenses on Nikon Z bodies. This proactive focus maintains consistency throughout your nocturnal photography voyage, as the camera resets focus upon power-up.

Transition to Manual Focus Mode

Once focus is established, transition your Nikon Z8 into manual focus mode. This strategic move preserves the precision of your focus setting, preventing inadvertent adjustments during your night photography pursuits.

Allocate a Custom Button for 100% Viewfinder Magnification

Streamline image review and focus refining by assigning a dedicated button on your Nikon Z8 to activate 100% viewfinder magnification. This speeds up the assessment of delicate features and allows you to fine-tune focus with accuracy.

Curate Personalized Settings within a Custom Menu Bank

Maximize the adaptability of your Nikon Z8 by creating and storing your preferred settings in a separate custom menu bank. This intentional move streamlines your workflow, providing quick access to the parameters that improve your night photography escapades.

CHAPTER NINETEEN
ADVANCED NIKON CAMERA TECHNIQUES
How to Shoot Using Continuous Shooting

Even the most skilled action shooter may miss critical moments, such as a pivotal defensive block during a football game or the cork falling off a baseball bat. This concern is alleviated by the continuous taking feature, which allows you to capture a succession of photos to help you remember the right moment or an interesting sequence of events. With the MB-D18 handle and EN-EL18b battery, the Nikon Z8 can shoot at an incredible 7 frames per second. This speed can be adjusted to nine frames per second. In Live View mode, you can utilize the electronic shutter to shoot silently at 15 or 30 frames per second, which is extremely fast. Continuous capturing is frequently associated with sports photography, although it has advantages outside of sports. One of the advantages is that it allows you to snap images or video clips that would be difficult to capture in single-shot mode. One issue is that you still need to filter through a lot of images to identify the ones that are preserved.

Still, the NIKON Z8's ability to shoot quickly comes in handy in some situations:

Fast-paced games require you to constantly shoot. However, it's crucial to realize that quick bursts of speed cannot compensate for unfavorable moments. At the fastest speed of 7 frames per second on the NIKON Z8, or 9/8 frames per second in CH/CL modes with the MB-D18 grip and EN-EL18b battery, a baseball traveling at 90 mph moves approximately 13 feet between frames. To capture the exact instant that a bat impacts a ball, you must be extremely skilled. When creating engaging scenes, continuous shooting shines since each frame contributes to the shots. When the camera is in continuous shooting mode, bracketing allows you to capture numerous images of the same scene. This makes it easier to select the optimal exposure or create high-dynamic range (HDR) images. With the NIKON Z8's high burst rate, bracketing and hand-held HDR shooting is simple and the software performs an excellent job of harmonizing slightly varied frames for the final design. Sequential capture is particularly useful for some subjects because the changes that occur between frames are minor yet significant. A few seconds can generate a variety of pictures of children playing, artists performing, models wearing clothing, or people moving about during an event. Furthermore, the optical sight allows for continual shooting, which is extremely handy. The NIKON Z8's huge buffer allows it to capture up to 200 images in a single burst. This is particularly true when utilizing fast memory cards such as the Sony G 64GB 400 MB/s

XQD or Sony G 64GB 299 MB/s SDXC. However, factors such as slower GPUs, RAW and JPEG input, and backup recording may all have an impact on performance. Choosing the appropriate frame rate is determined by the circumstances of the shot. When attempting to capture many exposures, proper planning and design are more crucial than taking continuous photos. Changing the frame rate to track the subject's motion improves multiple exposures.

Here are some suggested frame rates for different types of shooting:

7.0–9.0 fps: Ideal for sports and other fast-paced events requiring quick decision-making. For example, if you want to photograph lively children or catch their most captivating expressions for posterity, a high frame rate increases your chances of success. However, even at 7 frames per second, there is no guarantee that the key moment will not occur in between frames. For example, taking photographs at a Major League Baseball game. If you want to photograph a hitter, keep both eyes open and focus on the pitcher. Begin your action as soon as the bowler throws the ball, and try to catch it as the batter hits it. Even if the frame rate is quite high, like 7 frames per second, you may observe the bat-ball relationship between frames. This is because a 90-mph baseball travels 13 feet between shots. Recording multiple at-bats allows you to catch the critical moment of touch, whether it leads to a base hit or a foul ball.

4.0–6.0 fps: This range gives you options; you can change Custom Setting d1 to change the choices for Continuous Low Speed from 1 to 6 fps. For tasks with less fast-paced movements, lowering the frame rate is helpful. Also, choosing a slightly slower rate can help you keep the same shot speed when things like the speed of the card or the type of file might affect performance.

1.0–3.0 fps: The Continuous Low-Speed mode features slower frame rates, making it ideal for shooters who wish to snapshots swiftly but judiciously, so they don't fill up their memory cards with unnecessary photos. When set to 1 frame per second, you can shoot continuously by holding down the shutter button or taking small breaks by releasing it. Higher frame rates may unintentionally cause you to snap too many photos before deciding to stop. When bracketing, slower speeds are ideal. The NIKON Z8 can capture a three-frame bracket burst with a single shutter release. Rates like this are appropriate for subjects that shift or move in modest ways, such as models who hold the same position or look through some shots.

How to Shoot Using Super Speed Technique

The NIKON Z8 excels with high-speed photography, with catch rates of 15 and 30 frames per second. But it's crucial to understand the limitations that come with it. These fast speeds are only available in Live View mode and have some limitations, such as a time limit and a smaller image size. Using the NIKON Z8's automatic shutter in this mode makes the camera nearly silent, which is incredibly helpful while shooting at the insane speed of 30 photos per second.

Follow the easy steps below to turn on the fast speed mode:
- To get to Live View, make sure the live view switch, which is at 10 o'clock next to the Lv button, is set to the "still camera" position. To start live view mode, tap the Lv key.
- Pick Silent Live View Photography. Tap the "i" button to open the information menu, then go to the second page and find the Silent Live View Photography feature.
- Once Silent Live View Photography is marked, press OK and then choose SL1, SL2, or SL OFF. In SL1 and SL2 modes, you can take a single shot or keep shooting, but the multiple-exposure and long-exposure NR features will be turned off. When taken continuously, the settings for focus and brightness stay the same as they were for the first picture in the series. It's important to know that flicker or banding may happen when recording a live view in silence.

Now, let us analyze what makes Mode 1 and Mode 2 different:

Mode 1: Even if Custom Setting d1 is set at 4-6 frames per second, the CH release mode and CL mode can only go up to about 6 and 3 frames per second, respectively. You can select ISO settings ranging from Lo 1 to 25600. Mode 1 is intended for applications where low noise levels and little shutter movement are critical. This makes it ideal for photographing serene landscapes or elusive wildlife. To achieve the best results, set the camera on a stand to make it more stable.

Mode 2: It is recommended to use this mode in situations where you require quicker frame rates; however, it does come with a few drawbacks. When the Image Area is set to DX, which is 24 × 16mm, and the image quality is set to JPEG, the resulting photographs have dimensions of 3600 × 2400 pixels. During the Continuous Low and Quiet Continuous release modes, the NIKON Z8 is capable of shooting at a rate of 15 frames per second for a maximum of three seconds. This is sufficient time to snap forty-five photographs simultaneously. When it is set to Continuous High mode, it is capable of steadily shooting at a rate of 30 frames per second, which is sufficient for taking up to 90 photographs. Even though Mode 2 is cropped, it nevertheless provides you with extra "reach" for taking photographs of movement, which is especially useful when using long lenses. Despite this, it is essential to keep in mind that the mechanical shutter has the potential to produce distortion, particularly in situations when the subject is moving or the camera is actively panning. Imagine a scenario in which a runner runs a great distance between frames, resulting in visual distortion that gives the impression that the runner's limbs are not connected to their body. Particularly when there are sources of light that are moving quickly, it is essential to be mindful of distortion patterns such as color fringing, banding, moiré effects, and ragged edges.

Using the "A Tiny Slice of Time" Technique

A world of motion that is invisible to the naked eye can be revealed through the use of brief shots, which is an incredible phenomenon. It is incredible how quickly an electronic flash may put a stop to movement in an instant; flashes can reach rates of up to 1/50,000th of a second or even faster. The Nikon Z8 is equipped with an inbuilt flash unit that is capable of capturing fast-moving subjects; but, if you use an additional flash, such as the Nikon Speedlight, you will have even more alternatives to choose from. As a result of its shutter speeds that can reach as fast as 1/8,000th of a second, the NIKON Z8 is capable of successfully stopping practically any movement with unparalleled accuracy. Although such rapid camera speeds may not be required for the majority of shooting scenarios, there are certain circumstances in which they prove to be useful. When shooting in bright daylight with an aperture of f/1.8 and ISO 200, a shutter speed of 1/8,000th of a second is sufficient to maintain the desired level of brightness at lower sensitivity settings. The other side of the coin is that there are situations in which you require a faster shutter speed. It is recommended to use a slower shutter speed for many different types of sports and action photography settings. Subjects such as race cars, motorcycles, or helicopters are given the impression of dynamic motion as a result of this, and the blurring of wheels or wings makes the image appear more realistic.

When shooters start to use high-speed photography, they need to keep two important things in mind:

1. Adequate Lighting: Using very fast shutter speeds makes it easier to record exact moments in time, but they also make it much harder for light to reach the sensor. When you shoot at 1/8,000th second with an aperture of f/6.3, you need to set the ISO to 1600, even when it's daylight outside. When you use a smaller lens or a lower ISO setting, you need more light sources besides natural sun. Electronic flash units are the best choice for high-speed photos because they have both fast shutter speeds and the right amount of light.

2. High Shutter Speeds with Electronic Flash: In the course of daylight photography, it is difficult to resist the temptation to employ high shutter speeds in conjunction with electronic flash to freeze motion. On the other hand, the flash powers of the NIKON Z8 are restricted when particular conditions are accomplished. When the shutter speed is faster than 1/250th of a second, the camera will typically not allow you to use the flash in low-light settings. The maximum speed of the focal plane shutter is responsible for this limitation. This speed ensures that the flash only illuminates the portion of the sensor that is visible via the shutter slit when the shutter is functioning for the camera. It is no longer possible to use flash above this point as a result of this.

CHAPTER TWENTY

ABOUT THE NETWORK MENU

For cameras like the Nikon Z8, the network menu is an important part of how they work. Users can turn on and off airplane mode, connect to computers and smart devices, change Wi-Fi settings, and get to a lot of other useful options from this screen.

The Airplane Mode

Locate the settings window and choose the "ON" choice to turn off the camera's Bluetooth and Wi-Fi features. This action turns off both Bluetooth and Wi-Fi, which saves battery life and makes the camera safer by stopping people from getting into its network links without permission.

How to Connect Your Camera to a Smart Device

Bluetooth or Wi-Fi technology can be utilized to establish a connection between the camera and other electronic devices, such as smartphones and computers. Through the utilization of these wireless connection possibilities, the camera and gadgets that are acceptable for use together can function without any difficulties. The camera can be controlled from a distance, files can be shared, and other interesting functions may be utilized with ease thanks to this. You can instantly share images with others or start the shutter of the camera from a distance if you have a connection to Bluetooth and Wi-Fi. The whole user experience is enhanced as a result of this, as it provides you with additional creative choices with the camera.

Pairing Your Camera via Bluetooth

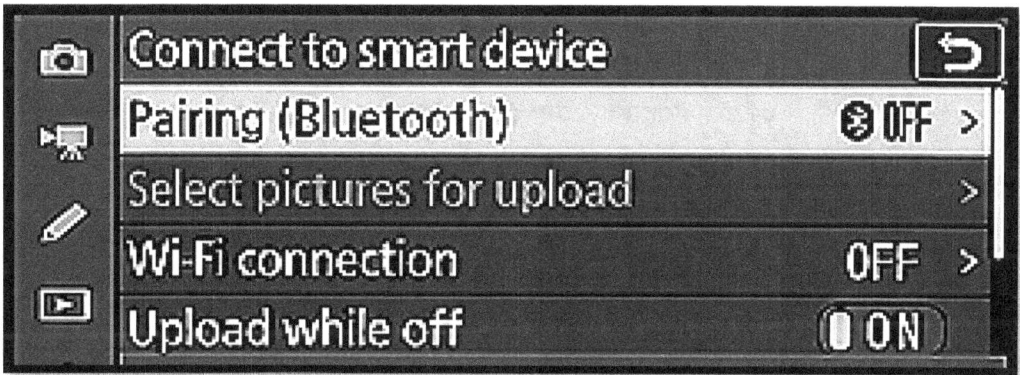

Use Bluetooth to connect the camera easily to suitable smart devices, which will make it more useful and flexible. Follow the steps below:

- **Press "Start pairing**": This will connect the camera to a suitable smart device. This will begin the pairing process and make it possible for the two devices to communicate easily and safely.
- **Paired devices:** Get a full list of all the smart devices that have already been paired, which makes the process of reconnecting them easier. Pick out a gadget from the list to join quickly and securely.
- **Bluetooth connection**: Enable Bluetooth by selecting the [ON] choice in the settings. This lets the camera easily connect to and stay connected to suitable devices.

Connecting Your Camera to an FTP Server

You can join FTP sites through Ethernet or wireless LAN, which increases the camera's networking options and makes data sharing easier.

1. **Network Settings**:
   - **Action**: Enhance your camera's connectivity by adding or modifying network settings. This will offer more control over connection options and improve overall functionality.
2. **Create Profile**:
   - **Action**: Set up new network profiles tailored to specific networking needs. This ensures optimized speed and flexibility based on your requirements.
3. **General Settings**:
   - **Action**: Customize personal names and password protection to secure your network. Adjust these settings to control who can access your network, enhancing both usability and security.
4. **Wireless Setup**:
   - **Action**: Configure wireless network settings:
     - **Infrastructure Mode**: Connect through routers for broader network access.
     - **Access-Point Mode**: Establish a direct connection between the camera and other devices.
     - **SSID & Channels**: Enter the SSID, select channels, and choose appropriate authentication/encryption methods and passwords for a stable Wi-Fi connection.
5. **TCP/IP Configuration**:

- o **Action**: Optimize infrastructure connections by manually setting IP addresses, ports, and DNS servers. This ensures more stable and reliable network operations.

6. **FTP Settings**:
   - o **Action**: Configure FTP settings:
     - **Server Type**: Select the correct server type and input the URL or IP address, target files, and port numbers.
     - **PASV Mode**: Enable PASV mode for secure file transfers.
     - **Private Login & Proxy Settings**: Adjust settings for private login and proxy servers to enhance data sharing security.
7. **Copy to and from Card**:
   - o **Action**: Transfer network profiles to and from memory cards for seamless sharing between devices. Ensure all devices have consistent network settings. To prevent unauthorized copying, secure profiles with passwords.

This guide provides a step-by-step approach to optimizing and securing your camera's network connectivity, ensuring efficient and safe data management.

How to connect to Other Cameras

Enable Synchronized Release:
- **Action**: Turn this feature ON to synchronize the shutter release across multiple cameras connected to the same network. This ensures coordinated shots and improves organization during multi-camera setups.

Network Settings:
- **Action**: Configure and expand your camera's network settings to add more options and improve handling flexibility. This helps in customizing the network experience to better suit your needs.

Create Profile:
- **Action**: Develop new network profiles to tailor the camera's networking configurations to your specific requirements. This ensures seamless operation and efficient data transfers.

General:
- **Action**: Adjust profile options to meet your preferences. Enhance security by encrypting profiles with passwords and renaming them as needed. Update password settings to control network access effectively.

TCP/IP:

- **Action**: Refine infrastructure connections using TCP/IP settings. Manually configure IP addresses for a more stable and reliable network, or choose automatic IP address assignment for simplicity.

Copy to/from Card:
- **Action**: Transfer network profiles to and from memory cards for easy sharing between devices:
    - **Copy from Card**: Import profiles from the root path of the memory card to the camera's profile list for convenient setup.
    - **Copy to Card**: Export camera profiles to the memory card, ensuring consistent network settings across different devices. Note that password-protected profiles cannot be copied to maintain security.

About the Camera USB Data Connection

Make sure the camera and other devices can join easily by making the appropriate changes through the USB data port.

- When connecting via USB to a PC or an Android device, make sure to choose the "MTP/PTP" choice for a successful link.
- If you want to use **NX MobileAir** with an iPhone, you must first select "iPhone" when linking with a USB-C to lightning connection from a different seller. For **NX MobileAir**-approved USB C to Lightning connections that work, check out the online help tools.
- If you want the highest possible performance while connecting the camera to a computer or another camera using an Ethernet wire that passes through a third-party USB-to-Ethernet adapter that is attached to the camera's USB data port, select [USB-LAN] as the connection type.

Note:
- When "iPhone" is chosen, the camera is set up to only talk to iPhones that have the NX MobileAir app installed. Choose MTP/PTP or USB-LAN if NX MobileAir is not being used.
- When you choose USB-LAN, the USB data port is only set up to work with USB-to-Ethernet connections. The port can't be used to connect to other devices via USB right now.

About the Router Frequency Band

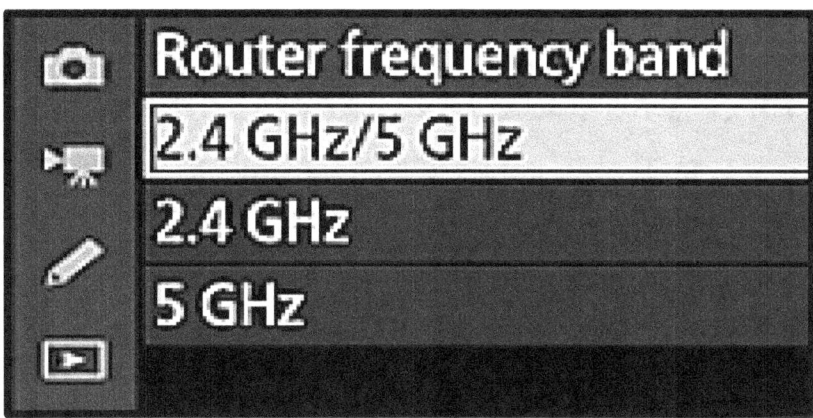

When connecting to a wifi network in infrastructure mode, make sure the link goes smoothly by picking the right band for the SSID. You can choose 2.4 GHz/5 GHz to connect to networks that use either of these bands, which work with a wide range of network setups and needs.

Here are some important things to also put into thought:

- During the time that it is looking for networks, the camera will only locate live networks that appear to be working on the band or bands that it has selected. This ensures that the network is recognized and that a connection is established on time.
- Band information, which shows either 2.4 GHz or 5 GHz, is easily shown next to the network's SSID, making it easy to choose a network.
- Picking 2.4 GHz/5 GHz lets you connect easily to wifi devices that can work on both bands. This complete list includes SSIDs that are present in the known bands, making it easier to choose a network and start a connection.

CHAPTER TWENTY-ONE

HOW TO CARE FOR THE CAMERA

How to Store/Keep the Camera for a Long-Term

Long-Term Storage: To prolong the life of the camera while it is not in use, do the following actions:

1. Take Out the Battery: After making sure the camera is off, take out the battery if it won't be used for a long time.

2. Environmental Considerations: It is important to keep the camera away from areas that have insufficient ventilation or excessive relative humidity (more than 60 percent). It is important to keep it away from the powerful electromagnetic fields that are produced by televisions and radios. It is also important to avoid extremely high temperatures, such as those that are higher than 50 degrees Celsius (122 degrees Fahrenheit) or lower than 20 degrees Celsius (4 degrees Fahrenheit).

Cleaning Techniques

Keeps the camera operating at peak efficiency by properly cleaning all of its parts:

1. Camera Body: Make use of a blower to remove any dust or lint, and then use a dry, soft cloth to gently wash the surface. After using the camera at the beach or in the ocean, wipe it out with a towel wet with distilled water and make sure it is completely dry.

2. Lens and Viewfinder: First, dust any lint using a blower. To get rid of stains and fingerprints, gently wipe the lens with a little bit of lens cleaning with a soft cloth.

3. Monitor: To avoid damaging the surface, use a chamois leather swab or soft cloth to carefully clean it after using a blower to remove any dust.

Cleaning of Image Sensors

Clean the sensor regularly to prevent dust particles from compromising the quality of the image:

- To remove dust, pick "**clean image sensor**" from the settings menu.
- To prevent breaking the delicate sensor while cleaning by hand, get advice from a Nikon-authorized service provider.

Using the Menus for Sensor Cleaning: To effectively clean your image sensor, follow these steps:

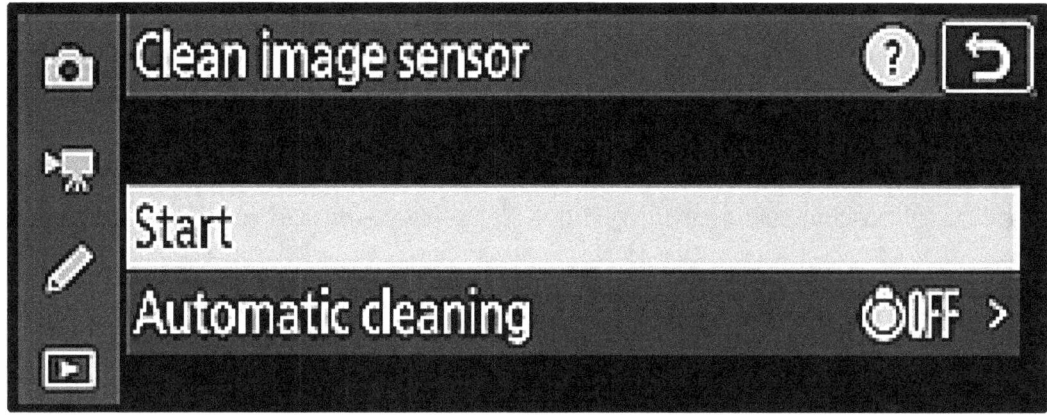

1. Move to "Settings" and choose "Clean image sensor."

2. Underline "Start" and make sure.

3. Don't switch off the camera or disrupt the cleaning process until it's finished.

4. For ease, the setup menu will be available after cleaning.

Cleaning the Sensor Manually: When manually cleaning the image sensor, use these steps:

1. Pick the option "Sensor shield stays open" from the setup menu.

2. After turning off the camera, take out the lens.

3. Check the sensor for any debris, and then blow away any dirt using a blower.

4. Steer clear of the sensor and, if needed, seek expert help.

Maintaining Image Sensor Accuracy: During the process of changing lenses or body covers, there is a concern that extraneous particles could fall into the camera and cause internal damage. These particles may adhere to the image sensor in certain shooting conditions, which will have an impact on the overall quality of the photograph. It is possible that even minute particles or lubricants that are created internally by the camera could pose a threat on rare occasions. Because of this, it is essential to exercise increased caution when replacing lenses or securing body covers, particularly in regions that are prone to dust. The body cap, lens mount, and camera mount should be thoroughly cleaned to remove any dust or foreign particles that may have become adhered to them. This will help to limit the likelihood of contamination.

Precautionary Measures when cleaning the Sensor: To protect the camera, heed these instructions:

1. Use Original Lens Caps: Whenever you remove a lens from your camera, be sure you replace the lens cap with the one that came with it. This easy procedure aids in preserving the integrity and cleanliness of the camera.

2. Options for Cleaning the Sensor: Manual cleaning is required if foreign matter is found on the image sensor and cannot be eliminated by the camera's built-in cleaning feature. To guarantee optimum performance, have your sensor thoroughly cleaned by Nikon-authorized service specialists.

3. Post-Processing Solutions: To rescue damaged images, investigate clean image alternatives offered in some photography apps when foreign matter impacts image quality.

Tips and Tricks for caring for your Camera

In this section is an all-inclusive camera maintenance guide:

Make cleanliness a priority

1. **Removing Dust and Debris**:
   - **Tools**: Use an air blower or blower brush.
   - **Action**: Gently blow air onto the camera body, lens, and accessories to dislodge any remaining dust and debris. This prevents particles from scratching the surfaces.
2. **Cleaning Smudges and Fingerprints**:
   - **Tools**: Microfiber cloth or lens-cleaning tissue.
   - **Action**: Lightly wipe the affected areas to remove lingering filth or fingerprints. Avoid applying excessive pressure to prevent damage.
3. **Lens Cleaning**:
   - **Tools**: Specialist lens cleaning solutions or wipes.
   - **Action**: Apply the cleaning solution to a lens-cleaning tissue or cloth. Gently clean the lens in circular motions to ensure even coverage and avoid streaks.
4. **Sensor Cleaning**:
   - **Action**: Exercise caution when cleaning the camera sensor. If needed, seek professional sensor cleaning services or refer to the camera's manual for proper cleaning techniques.

Following these steps will help maintain your camera equipment in optimal condition, ensuring clear, sharp images and extending the lifespan of your gear.

Preventive Measures

- To avoid dust, fingerprints, and scratches, always use a lens cap while the lens is not in use.- For secure storage and transit, spend money on a high-quality camera bag that fits your camera model and provides enough padding and protection.

Control Environmental Exposure

- To avoid performance deterioration and internal component damage, abide by the suggested temperature ranges specified in the camera handbook.
- Steer clear of high humidity areas to avoid condensation development and give the camera time to adjust while moving between severe temperatures.

UV Filter Usage

- To protect your lens from UV rays, scratches, and contaminants, think about using a UV filter.- Choose filters with many coatings to reduce reflection-related visual artifacts and make sure they work with the diameter of your lens.

Handle and Treat Your Camera with Care

1. **Ensure Stability**:
   - **Action**: Keep a firm grip on the camera to minimize shaking and ensure stability during shooting. This helps achieve sharp, clear images and reduces the likelihood of camera shake.
2. **Lens Attachment and Removal**:
   - **Action**: Handle lenses with care when attaching or removing them. Avoid applying excessive force to prevent damage to the lens or the camera mount. Always align the lens properly with the mount to ensure a secure connection.
3. **Avoid Sensor Contact**:
   - **Action**: Refrain from touching the camera sensor, as it is a delicate component that can be easily damaged. If you suspect that the sensor needs cleaning, seek professional assistance to avoid causing harm.

By following these practices, you can maintain your camera's performance and longevity while ensuring the safe and effective use of your equipment.

Battery Maintenance

Use Original Batteries:
- **Action**: Ensure optimum performance and safety by using only original Nikon batteries specifically designed for the Z8 camera. This ensures compatibility and reliability.

Follow the Charging Instructions:
- **Action**: Charge batteries according to the manufacturer's guidelines. Avoid exposing them to direct sunlight or extreme temperatures, which can affect their performance and lifespan.

Monitor Battery Health:
- **Action**: Regularly check the performance of your batteries. Replace any batteries that show signs of leakage or rapid degradation to prevent potential damage to your camera and ensure reliable operation.

Updates for Firmware

- Keep up with the most recent firmware updates for the Nikon Z8 to get access to new features, improvements, and problem fixes.

- To ensure smooth upgrades, download firmware updates from Nikon's official website or software applications, and then follow the installation instructions.

Safe Storage and Transportation

- To evade leaks, take out the batteries before keeping the camera in storage for a long time.
Keep the camera dry, clean, and dust-free; if moisture is a concern, think about using humidity-controlled storage options.
- When traveling, protect your photographic equipment from shocks and bumps by using a well-padded backpack or case.

Continuous Maintenance

- Plan routine maintenance and repairs by service providers approved by Nikon to protect camera performance and take care of any problems.
- For suggested servicing intervals and maintenance instructions specific to your camera model, consult experts or consult the camera manual.

Battery Maintenance Tips

The following recommendations will help your rechargeable Nikon EN EL15c batteries work to their fullest potential:
Avoid Frequent Power Cycling:
- **Action**: Minimize frequent power cycling when the battery is fully depleted. This practice helps extend the battery's lifespan. Always ensure batteries are fully charged before reuse.

Replace Weak Batteries:
- **Action**: If the battery's capacity drops significantly after a full charge and use at room temperature, consider replacing it with a new rechargeable battery.

Do Not Overcharge:

- **Action**: Avoid charging batteries that are already fully charged to prevent potential performance issues.

Insulate Terminals Before Recycling:
- **Action**: Before recycling rechargeable batteries, insulate their terminals as per local regulations to ensure safe disposal.

Avoid Interference During Charging:
- **Action**: Keep the battery and charger still and do not touch them while charging. Stop using the charger immediately if any irregularities occur.

Maintain Clean Connections:
- **Action**: Regularly clean battery connections to avoid performance issues caused by contamination.

Use Batteries Promptly:
- **Action**: Use charged batteries as soon as possible to prevent power drain over time.

Battery Compatibility:
- **Action**: EN-EL15c batteries can be swapped with EN-EL15b and EN-EL15a batteries if necessary. However, note that EN-EL15b and EN-EL15a batteries may offer fewer captures per charge compared to EN-EL15c.

CHAPTER TWENTY-TWO

TROUBLESHOOTING PROBLEMS ON THE Z8

All devices are prone to problems, including the Nikon Z8. The following are typical problems that come up while troubleshooting the Nikon Z8:

The Z8 cannot be Powered ON

If you are unable to get your Nikon Z8 camera to turn on, attempt the following troubleshooting steps:

Check Battery Placement and Charge:
- **Action**: Ensure the battery is properly inserted and fully charged. Verify that it is correctly seated in the camera.

Inspect for Dirt or Debris:
- **Action**: Examine the battery connectors and camera contacts for any dirt or debris that might hinder proper connection. Clean gently if needed.

Test with a Different Battery:
- **Action**: Try using a different battery, preferably from another brand, to see if the camera powers on. This helps determine if the issue is with the battery itself.

Seek Professional Help:
- **Action**: If the camera still does not turn on, visit an authorized repair shop or contact Nikon customer service for further assistance. They can provide expert support and repair services.

Autofocus Issues

The performance of your camera might be greatly impacted by autofocus problems. Try the following fixes if you're having trouble staying focused:

1. Check the lens's location to make sure the autofocus switch is in the "AF" (autofocus) position.

2. Confirm that the appropriate autofocus mode (such as Single AF or Continuous AF) is chosen by going to the camera's menu and going over the focus mode settings.

3. Make sure the lens contacts are firmly fastened to the camera body and give them a thorough cleaning.

4. Certify that the firmware on your camera is current; updates often bring with them better-focusing capabilities.

5. Consider sending the camera and lens to an approved service center for calibration or repair if the issue continues.

Problems with Image Quality

Try these troubleshooting actions if you see a drop in picture quality or run into other image-related problems:

1. Confirm again that the ISO, white balance, and picture adjustments on your camera are appropriate for the shooting environment.
   - Ensure the ISO is adjusted correctly for the available light.
   - For correct color reproduction, adjust the white balance to match the surrounding light.
   - Check that picture parameters like sharpness, saturation, and contrast are set up to get the results you want.

2. To clean the picture sensor, use a sensor cleaning tool made especially for your camera type. Also, carefully follow the camera's manual to properly and non-damagingly remove dust and debris from the sensor.

3. Check the lens carefully for any possible flaws that can influence the quality of the picture, such as smudges, dirt, or scratches.
- Gently wipe the lens surface with a microfiber cloth or a lens cleaning solution to get rid of any impurities.
- For best results, pay close attention to the front and back lens components.

4. Update the firmware on your camera using the most recent version that Nikon provides.
- Frequently check the Nikon software programs or official website for firmware upgrades.
- Bug fixes and enhancements that might improve picture quality and solve a variety of problems are often included in firmware upgrades.

5. If you are still experiencing issues with the quality of your photographs, you may wish to contact Nikon's customer support or visit one of their authorized service facilities to receive additional assistance. A specialist is also able to discover and fix any underlying issues that may be present in your camera system, ensuring that your photographs are of the highest possible quality and functioning.

Error Messages

Error messages might represent several camera-related problems, each of which has to be resolved differently.

This is a thorough collection of typical error messages along with possible fixes:

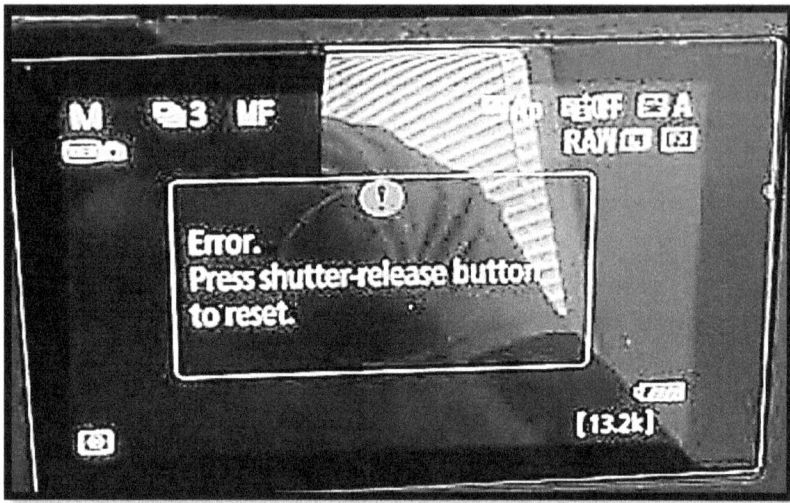

1. Err" Message: This usually indicates a possible issue with the camera. Try taking the battery out and putting it back in, making sure it is well charged. For help, get in touch with Nikon's customer care if the problem continues.

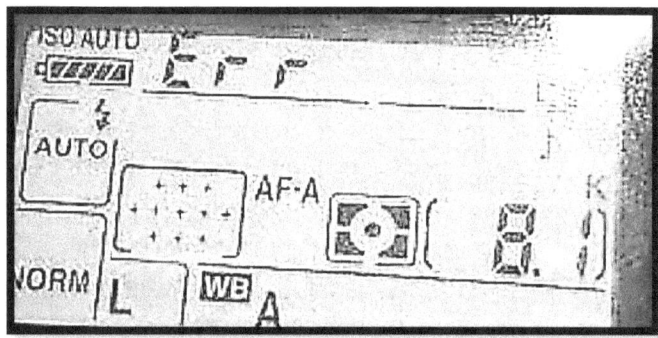

2. Card is full or Card Cannot be Read Message: To properly reply to the "Card is full" or "Card cannot be read" message, it is imperative that the memory card be correctly placed into the camera. Should the issue continue, think about getting a new memory card or formatting the one you already have (keep in mind that formatting removes all of the data from the card).

3. "Lens not attached" message: Check to make sure the lens is fastened to the camera body firmly. Make sure the lens snaps securely into place when replacing it after removing it.

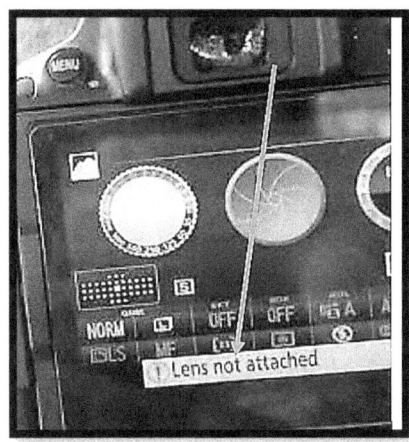

4. **Battery Exhausted Message:** If the notice "Battery exhausted" appears, you should either make use of a battery that has been fully charged or charge the battery that is already installed. If the problem persists, the battery may need to be replaced.

5. **No Memory Card Message:** Make sure the required memory card is placed into the camera to avoid receiving the "No memory card" message. To guarantee a correct connection, take it out and put it back in if it has previously been entered.

6. **The "Lens error" Message:** Suggests that there could be a problem with the lens mechanism. Turn the camera on and off a few times. If the issue still exists, take the lens off and reconnect it firmly. Seek expert help if the mistake continues.

7. **File cannot be Played Message:** To prevent the "File cannot be played" message from appearing on your screen, check that the file format is compatible with your recording device. Attempt to play the file on a device that is suited for it, or convert the file format if it is required.

8. **System Error Message:** Try returning the camera to its factory settings if you get the "System error" message.

9. **"Lens aperture ring not set to minimum aperture" Message**: Set the lens's aperture ring to the minimum value (often denoted by an "A" or a number). See the lens handbook for instructions if the problem continues.

10. **"Memory card write protected" Message**: It is important to check that the write-protection switch on the memory card is in the protected position. If this is the case, you should change it to the unlocked situation. If the problem continues, you might want to think about using an alternative memory card. Note: It's always advisable to get help from Nikon's customer support or authorized repair centers if you keep getting error messages or don't know how to fix them.

Issues with Connectivity

Try these troubleshooting steps if you're having difficulty connecting your Nikon Z8 to other devices or if you're having problems with wireless functionality:
Enable Wi-Fi and Bluetooth:
- **Action**: Ensure that both Wi-Fi and Bluetooth are enabled on your camera. Navigate to the settings menu and confirm that these features are turned on and configured correctly.

Check Device Compatibility:
- **Action**: Verify that the device you're trying to connect with meets the necessary standards and protocols required for compatibility with your camera. Consult the user manual or the device's specifications for detailed compatibility information.

Update Firmware:
- **Action**: Check that your camera has the latest firmware version installed. Firmware updates often include performance improvements and bug fixes that can enhance connection stability. Visit Nikon's official website to download and install any available firmware updates for your camera model.

Refer to the User Manual:
- **Action**: Consult the camera's user manual for specific instructions on setting up Wi-Fi or troubleshooting connection issues. The manual provides model-specific guidance and step-by-step instructions.

Contact Customer Support:
- **Action**: If you continue to experience issues, contact Nikon's customer support for additional assistance. Provide detailed information about the problem you're encountering. Nikon's support team may offer further troubleshooting advice or direct you to an authorized service center if needed.

Overheating

The Nikon Z8 camera may overheat if used for extended periods, which might cause a warning and perhaps impair functionality.

Take into account the following fixes to deal with this problem:
1. Avoid Extreme Conditions: Reduce the amount of time spent using cameras in areas that are very hot or brightly lit. Shooting in colder settings may help reduce the chance of overheating since high temperatures can compound the problem.
2. Disable Unnecessary Functions: Turn off any unnecessary camera features, as they may add to the strain and cause overheating. This includes features such as

continuous shooting, long exposure noise reduction, and photo preview. Overheating can be avoided by reducing the pressure on the camera.

3. Allow for Cooling Periods: If an overheating warning occurs, immediately turn off the camera and remove the battery for a few minutes to allow it to cool completely. To prevent the camera from overheating more, wait until it has reached a safe working temperature before using it.

4. Use External Cooling: To improve airflow around the camera during extended shooting sessions, think about using an external fan or other cooling equipment. By doing so, heat may be dispersed more efficiently and overheating problems can be avoided.

Quick Battery Drain

If your Nikon Z8's battery life is rapidly declining do the following actions to fix the problem:

1. Use Original Nikon Accessories: Ensure that the batteries and chargers you use are genuine Nikon products. Incompatible or counterfeit batteries may not work as well as they should and can cause the battery to deplete more quickly.

2. Optimize Power-Consuming features: Look for and reduce the usage of settings or features that use a lot of power, including long-term LCD screen use or continuous focusing. During photo shoots, using these parameters might assist prolong battery life.

3. Customize Auto Power-Off Settings: You can lower the amount of time the camera stays idle before entering sleep mode by changing the auto power-off settings in the camera menu. This can help prevent unnecessary power waste during the camera's idle period.

4. Check Battery Contacts: Make sure the battery contacts are clear of dirt, clean, and oriented correctly by looking at them on both the battery and the camera body. Power problems may arise from rusted or dirty connections interfering with the battery connection.

5. Consider Battery Replacement: If troubleshooting does not cure the problem, you might want to consider purchasing a new battery. Batteries can deteriorate and lose their ability to hold a charge over time. If you continue to experience battery depletion, contact Nikon's customer service for extra advice and direction on how to solve the problem.

Issues with SD Cards

Problems with your SD cards might result in annoying problems such as write errors, data loss, or other issues. To fix such problems, do the following actions:

1. Verify Formatting and Compatibility: To start with, make sure the SD card you're using is appropriately formatted and compatible with your device. Problems may often arise from incorrect formatting or compatibility difficulties.

2. Format the SD Card: To ensure better compatibility and functionality, format the SD card using your device's formatting option. Remember that formatting will destroy all data from the card, so before proceeding, make sure you have a backup of any critical information.

3. Address Error Messages: If your camera displays an error warning about the SD card, consider plugging it into a computer and using disk repair or formatting software to remedy any potential file system issues. If there is no specific error notification, there may be a corruption issue with the camera itself.

4. Select High-Quality SD Cards: If you want to lower your chance of data corruption or other issues, think about purchasing SD cards from reliable and respectable manufacturers. Better cards are less likely to have performance or compatibility problems.

5. Replace or Seek Assistance: It could be required to swap out the SD card for a new one if the issue doesn't go away after trying several fixes or if the card is physically damaged. As an alternative, get in touch with Nikon customer support for further help and direction in fixing the problem.

Issues with the Firmware or Software

The procedures to deal with these kinds of issues are as follows:

1. Look for Firmware upgrades: Visit the Nikon website to see whether your camera has any firmware upgrades available. Updating the firmware may often enhance functionality and solve a variety of problems with the camera's overall performance.

2. Do a Factory Reset: If changing the firmware does not resolve the issue, try performing a factory reset on the camera. Refer to the user manual to understand how to start a factory reset. This removes all individual setups and resets the camera to its default settings. This can help to resolve issues with program settings or glitches.

3. Seek Professional Assistance: If you're still having problems with any of the camera's features or settings, such as menu navigation or button response, you should contact Nikon's customer support or visit an approved service center. They may offer professional assistance and troubleshooting solutions targeted to your specific issues.

INDEX

193

E

O

211

www.ingramcontent.com/pod-product-compliance
Lightning Source LLC
Chambersburg PA
CBHW082232220526
45479CB00005B/1210